You cannot cast out the flesh; it must be crucified. In *Wake Up Dead*, Jenny Donnelly unpacks what it means to die daily and how this practice—like a seed planted in the ground—leads to realizing one's untapped potential.

John Bevere
Best-selling Author and Minister
Co-founder of Messenger International & MessengerX

Wake Up Dead will be one of my go-to study guides for victorious Christian living. I have watched Jenny die to her will on so many levels. The Apostle Paul said we must die *daily*. It's not a one-time event. It's a daily decision to pick up my cross and follow my Lord. Thank you, Jenny, for living a life of death to self.

Callie Gray
Pastor, Her Voice National Prayer Leader

In her book, *Wake Up Dead*, Jenny Donnelly has done a phenomenal job of capturing the secret of unlimited life potential and fearless foresight. Jesus told us in Luke 17:33, "Whoever seeks to save his life will lose it, but whoever will lose his life for My sake, will find it." In this book, *Wake Up Dead*, Jenny has captured the words to shift our thinking, re-evaluate our navigation processes in life and emerge with a bold new understanding of how to live and accomplish goals without the mental roadblocks that keep us imprisoned in our thinking. As you read *Wake Up Dead*, you will find the limitations you've placed on yourself fade away, creating new vision, new pathways, new broad fields, and powerful freedom to accomplish everything you are on this earth to do in life. Proverbs 23:7 says, "As a man thinks in his heart, so is he." Get ready to be free from the confining cocoon and take flight into the amazing freedom we are designed to live in.

Cindy McGill
Founder of Hope for the Harvest Ministries and Freedom Lounge Outreaches
Author of *What Your Dreams Are Telling You: Unlocking Solutions While You Sleep* and *Words That Work: A Language of Light for a World Living In Darkness.*
www.cindymcgill.org

"By reading this book, you will understand that real freedom comes from letting go of anything that God doesn't have for you. You must trust the process! It will feel counterintuitive to let go of your life in order to gain true life. *Wake Up Dead* is a bold invitation to all people who want to rise victorious in every area of life! "

Brooke Thomas
Entrepreneur, Business Coach, Speaker, Founder of Live Out Loud

The scripture says, "My old self has been crucified with Christ. It is no longer I who live, but Christ lives in me." Jenny lives her life this way. Her book, *Wake Up Dead*, will literally teach you how to find true life in Christ. This book has the potential to change your life forever if you will allow God to point you toward the real truth of God's Word.

Danny McDaniel
Pastor, Social Entrepreneur, Author

WAKE UP DEAD

JENNY DONNELLY

TETELESTAI
PUBLISHING

Wake Up Dead: Dying To Self To Experience True Life
Copyright © 2021 Tetelestai Ministries.

All rights reserved. Printed in the United States of America. No part of this book may be used or reproduced in any manner whatsoever without written permission except in the case of brief quotations embodied in critical articles or reviews. Requests for permission should be directed to www.TetelestaiMinistries.com

Published by Tetelestai Ministries, Portland

Scripture quotations marked TPT are from The Passion Translation®. Copyright © 2017, 2018 by Passion & Fire Ministries, Inc. Used by permission. All rights reserved. ThePassionTranslation.com.

Scripture quotations marked NIV are taken from the Holy Bible, New International Version®, NIV®. Copyright © 1973, 1978, 1984, 2011 by Biblica, Inc.™ Used by permission of Zondervan. All rights reserved worldwide. www.zondervan.comThe "NIV" and "New International Version" are trademarks registered in the United States Patent and Trademark Office by Biblica, Inc.™

Scripture quotations marked NLT are taken from the Holy Bible, New Living Translation, copyright ©1996, 2004, 2015 by Tyndale House Foundation. Used by permission of Tyndale House Publishers, Carol Stream, Illinois 60188. All rights reserved.

Scriptures marked THE VOICE are taken from the THE VOICE (The Voice): Scripture taken from THE VOICE ™. Copyright© 2008 by Ecclesia Bible Society. Used by permission. All rights reserved.

Editor: Pauline Wick
Book design: Rachel Plyler
Cover design: Jenny Donnelly, Tiffanee Cummings, Rachel Plyler
ISBN: 9781637904633

First Edition: October 2021
10 9 8 7 6 5 4 3 2 1

*Oh, if only I could be completely done with my dead self!
If only I never felt nerves of disdain again,
or argued with God about my insecurities.
Until then, I will continue to let the scared, brittle, doubtful part of me
break away through pressure and darkness
and celebrate the power of Christ that bursts out of
my surrendered and pathetic places.*

CONTENTS

Introduction   13

PART 1: DYING TO SELF - A STARTING PLACE

1. A Dangerous Prayer   21
2. Crushing   27
3. The Death - Life Paradox   37
4. Weekend At Bernie's   43
5. Dead Man Talking   51
6. Die To Multiply   61
7. Dying "Quick Reference"   69
8. The Most Important Part   85

PART 2: EXPERIENCING TRUE LIFE - PLACES TO DIE

9. Dying to Dignity   93
10. Dying to Pride in Marriage   101
11. Dying to Pride in Parenting   109
12. Dying to Calling, Career, and Finances   121
13. Dying to Counterfeit Comfort   131
14. Dying to Strengths and Gifting   145

PART 3: WARFARE - LAY DOWN TO RISE UP

15. Warrior, Rise Up	161
16. Worship	169
17. Wounds Forgiven	177
18. The Word	187
19. Weapons - WARdrobe Part 1	199
20. Weapons - WARdrobe Part 2	209
21. Our Warrior, The Holy Spirit	217
22. Win The War	227
23. Wake Up to True Life	237
Appendix	241

I BELIEVE YOU WILL BE A TOTALLY DIFFERENT PERSON BY THE TIME YOU ARE DONE READING THIS BOOK.

INTRODUCTION

My oldest daughter was eight years old when she proudly picked out her first authentic American Girl Doll. If you are familiar with these dolls, they are famous for their quality, nostalgia, and their price tag! Little girls can choose a look-alike doll that mirrors her own features, which is exactly what Hannah did. With a giant smile on her face and a twinkle in her eyes, Hannah walked out of the Seattle American Girl store with her very own blonde-haired, blue-eyed doll.

A few months later, I was cleaning out her closet and saw this beloved doll upside down in the corner, disheveled and forgotten about. Trying to erase the price tag of this doll from my memory, I picked her up and combed my fingers through her snarled blonde hair. I looked for a more proper place to put her in Hannah's room and decided I would enforce that this doll be enjoyed.

As I held her in my hands and straightened out her clothes,

God spoke to my spirit *clearly*. I'll never forget it.

"*This is how some people treat me. When they meet me, they want me to take on their image instead of them taking on my image. They bring me out to play when I can entertain them, but I get put away when they are bored with me. My value is often forgotten about.*"

I didn't know quite what to do with this, but it grieved me. I knew it was true. Some of us have become Christians thinking that Jesus is going to jump on *our train*, follow *our dreams*, commit to *our plans*, and somehow become *our self-help guru*.

Is this the gospel message? No, it is absolutely the opposite!

DYING TO LIVE

Have you ever wondered, *Is there more to life than this?*

The world offers us fame and fortune as our ultimate happiness. Ask anyone who has actually achieved it. If they don't have God I can promise you, they are still searching for more. The world cannot satisfy the deepest places within us. Seeking satisfaction from the world is like drinking soda trying to quench our thirst. We might have the volume of liquid in our guts, but our cells aren't being hydrated so we're still left feeling dry after all that drinking!

So it is with the world's offer for deep meaning and purpose. Most of us have heard it and it's true: there is a God-sized hole in our hearts that only *he* can satisfy.

If you've been trying to fill the hole in your heart with anything besides God, you're reading the right book. If you've been feeling restless, hopeless, empty, or fighting bouts of depression and anxiety, you're reading the right book. If you've been experiencing emotions or behaviors that are choking out your joy and satisfaction, you're reading the right book.

Maybe you are a person who loves God and you simply want to get as close as you possibly can to him. You're reading the right book. Perhaps you're facing a huge life change and you're being forced to let go of what you *thought* life would look like. You're reading the right book.

No matter which one of these describes you the best, we all start here: letting go of our lives and clinging to Christ. Jesus said if we give up our life, surrender it all to him, and love him first and most, we get true life!

> "Those who cling to their lives will give up true life. But those who let go of their lives for my sake and surrender it all to me will discover true life!"
>
> Matthew 10:39 TPT

In this surrendered life, we openly and intentionally take on the new life of Christ within. We don't look the same! We begin to take on his nature, his image, his motives, and his plans. Our paradigms and plans get washed away in exchange for his blueprints for our lives. We trust him with a totally different life and declare wholeheartedly, "Wherever you are going, I will follow."

There is going to be a time when we will be faced with choices and challenges that we haven't yet had to wrestle with, especially as Americans who are used to forming lives that work well for us and cater to our comforts. If we have only seen Jesus as our entertainment or "look-alike doll," we are going to be unfit to make the right decision when the time comes.

The Bible says to let go of the tight grip we have on our own self-centered lives in exchange for *true life* that is only found in Christ! It is an extreme message: we will triumph *if* we do not love and cling to our own lives, even when faced with death.

> They conquered him completely through the blood of the Lamb and the powerful word of his testimony.
> They triumphed because they did not love and cling to

their own lives, even when faced with death.

Revelation 12:11 TPT

Look at these *powerful* words that Jesus spoke:

> "The person who loves his life and pampers himself will miss true life! But the one who detaches his life from this world and abandons himself to me, will find **true life** and enjoy it forever! If you want to be my disciple, **follow me and you will go where I am going**. And if you truly follow me as my disciple, the Father will **shower his favor upon your life**."
>
> John 12: 25-26 TPT (emphasis added)

This is really good news. Let's review:
Detach.
Abandon.
Find true life.
Enjoy it forever.
Follow me.
Go where I am going.
Shower favor upon your life.

Do you want the favor of God? Do you want to experience true life? Or, would you rather experience a counterfeit version of the life that you were supposed to live? Of course you want true life! To find it, you must follow *him*.

I believe that this book is preparation for your future. As I share my stories, you will recognize areas in your own life where you are trying to do things your own way, some areas you probably don't even realize. As you take the challenge to die alongside me, you will find yourself experiencing more internal breakthrough and fulfillment. Trust me when I tell you this!

There are a few significant exercises throughout the book that will help you experience radical growth. You will be given the option to go through most of the exercises with me audibly by using the QR code printed at the beginning of each exercise (a link will appear when you place your phone camera over the top of the QR image). You can return to these exercises as often as you like.

I believe that this book has the ability to catapult you into a totally new life - true life! One that is far more fulfilling than the one you might have planned for yourself.

To wake up dead means you will open your eyes in the morning alive to the good news that your life, your day, your children, your business, your finances (and more!) are not your own.

I believe you will be a totally different person by the time you are done reading this book.

Holy Spirit, I pray for every single person reading this book to trust you, to let go of themselves, and to be raised up to true life. In Jesus' name, amen.

PART 1

DYING TO SELF

A STARTING PLACE

LORD, LET ME NOT BE THE SAME PERSON A YEAR FROM NOW. MAKE ME INTO NEW WINE.

1

A DANGEROUS PRAYER

In the fall of 2018, I prayed a dangerous prayer:
"Lord, let me not be the same person a year from now. Make me into new wine."

We had just put the second Her Voice Conference on the schedule and I knew I didn't want to serve these women old bread. In fourteen months, I wanted God to serve them something fresh; something new. As the leader of the organization, this meant that *I* would have to be new.

I remember thinking, *God has fourteen whole months to make me into new wine! This seems like ample time.*

What I hadn't considered was the process by which new wine is made: crushing.

CRUSHING, COMMENCE

It started with a strange dream.

My dead body lay in front of me, cold, purple, and lifeless. Three doctors were carefully and urgently hovering over my dead body. They had no interest in bringing me back to life. No, they were only concerned about one thing: removing a living baby from my lifeless body!

A beautiful, rose-colored baby was tucked safely in the amniotic sack. The doctors were carefully trying to remove the baby and somehow I knew this baby would only live if the sac remained intact.

Standing there watching this take place, I became extremely concerned that the doctors wouldn't be able to remove the baby without puncturing the sac. Looking up to heaven, I prayed with everything in me, *God, let this baby live!* I began to travail in prayer for the doctors. Everything in me was thrusted toward heaven! I was so desperate for this baby to live.

I didn't care one single ounce that I was dead.

ARE YOU DEAD YET?

Soon after this dream, I was on the phone with a minister who is gifted at dream interpretation. He said, "Jenny, dreams of being dead aren't bad. Actually, they can be quite good. Jesus calls us to die to ourselves so that we can live in him. I guess the question is, 'Are you dead yet?'"

"Since God gave me a dream about it, (sigh) my guess is 'no.'"

I got off of the phone understanding that this dream was an invitation to die to myself. Still, I had the sense that there was more to this dream than a personal invitation.

I knew I needed to unpack this dream. Dreams are incredible

because they *reveal* in our sleep what we're *unaware of* when we're awake.

This motivated me to ask the Holy Spirit more questions: *"Why three doctors, and what was significant about the amniotic sac?"*

I believe the three doctors symbolize the Father, Son, and Holy Spirit. Their care for this baby's survival told me how important the creation and survival of this baby was to God and all of heaven.

What about that sac? Why did it have to remain intact?

Leaning on my kitchen island, I pulled up my phone and typed in the browser, "baby born in amniotic sac" and here is what I found:

> *The amniotic membrane enclosing a fetus is called the CAUL [kôl].*
>
> *The "en-caul" birth occurs when the infant is born inside the entire amniotic sac.*
>
> *"En" means "within"*
>
> *"En Caul" means "within the Caul"*

My spirit leapt! The Holy Spirit dropped a message in me at that very moment. Put into words, it would read similar to this:

I WANT TO BIRTH A NEW YOU WITHIN YOUR CALLING.

> *"I'm bringing forth new life within you, just as you have asked. However, I don't just want to birth something new in you, I want to birth a new you within your CALLING (en caul-ing). When I bring forth new life, I do it within a person's calling. In order for this to happen, you will need to be dead."*

HURRY UP AND DIE

This lead me to my next question: *How does one pursue dying to self?*

Ignorantly, I figured the best way to activate this would be for him to give me a list of all of the areas of my life where I was selfish, prideful, doubtful, deceived, wounded, and insecure.

"Okay, Lord, where do I need to die? What does that look like? Is it a prayer? Is it a person I need to forgive? An attitude? A motive? Just tell me all the things and I'll die the best I can. I'm no die-to-self expert, but I know there will be pain involved, so let's just get this over with."

Well, that didn't work. Even though I asked for the list, he wouldn't comply. Like a good friend who wouldn't fire hose you with all the things you're really failing at, he wouldn't point out all of my flaws either. Not only that, my sense was that he had a different plan altogether.

After asking the question, *"Lord, where do I need to die?"* all I could sense in response were these words delivered in a loving tone…

"You'll see."

I HAD NO IDEA THAT THIS EXPERIENCE WOULD BECOME THE HAMMER TO CRUSH THINGS IN ME THAT NEEDED TO DIE.

2

CRUSHING

Sitting on the edge of a bed, a seasoned minister, Ms. Jackie, sat with me privately as I told her of the betrayal. She responded, "Oh, yes. I can see the pain. That is really deep." She could see the hurt and pain sitting deep in me with her spiritual eyes.

She walked me through verbally forgiving a close friend. As the words came out of my mouth, she would say, "Go a little deeper." She used soft and encouraging words to help me go from an intellectual "heady" place to a place where I could feel my heart. That meant feeling the pain!

Months earlier, I had encountered one of the most deceptive betrayals of my life. A friend I was once very close with had spun lies about my husband and me through a group of our friends and the church that we co-pastor.

During this time, my body had broken down in many different ways and I was in a lot of pain. At one point, I was in so much pain I didn't want to live anymore. It was horrific.

Meanwhile, my mind was racing, trying to think of how this relationship had turned sour. I wanted to fix it, but God was allowing this friendship to be crushed to pieces. Somewhere along the way, I realized that this relationship could not be salvaged. People were leaving our church and our friend group because they were trying to figure out what they believed.

Now, here I sat with a loving minister, helping me in this crushing moment. I didn't know what to do with the pain. I had lost friends and been lied about. My body was in excruciating pain. I was beyond desperate for help.

Ms. Jackie explained something to me that has forever changed my life. She explained that forgiving others includes letting go of the LOSS. The loss of what I wanted it to be. The loss of a friendship. The loss of trust. The loss of intimacy.

That loss within me felt like a cinderblock sitting heavy in my gut. She explained that when we forgive, we give over the loss. We let it go. We hand it to Christ.

That's when I began to wail from the pit of my soul. As soon as I could cry from that hidden and dark place of pain, it was like a crane reached into the deep and pulled that cinderblock of pain and hurt up and out of my body. It came out through *wailing*.

This is a key to getting free from this kind of heartache: we must access that place of pain and judgment that we've held against others and empty ourselves of it by giving it to Christ!

Releasing people from our hearts is one of the most difficult things to do because our pride wants to hang on to the hurt (as if it will protect us from getting hurt again)! Maybe we just want to control the outcome? Either way, I had to find this pain, which wasn't available intellectually, and access it deep within me.

As I connected with the loss and the tears and grief poured from within me, I could feel the weight of pain and poison from betrayal leave my body.

She had to be released from my heart in order to be released from my life.

The old Jenny would've thought, *Now that I feel better and my heart is free, I have enough love to recover this friendship.* This would have been done in complete disobedience to God! He said it was *over*, so Jenny had to let go of (die to) her own desired outcomes.

After my heart was free of the pain, I was able to end this friendship in one intentional conversation. With apologies and forgiveness, I did what was right in the eyes of God and health to my bones. It wasn't fun. It wasn't pleasant. It wasn't anything I would ever want to do again. But it was what God asked me to do: *"Let her go."*

LETTING GO LEADS TO NEW LIFE

At the time, I had no idea that this pain was connected to making me into new wine. I just thought I was going through hell. I had no idea that this experience would become the hammer to crush things in me that needed to die:

My lack of boundaries… *crushed.*

My desire to have people know the truth about me… *crushed.*

My fear of confrontation… *crushed.*

My fear of disappointing people… *crushed.*

Out of this dying place, there was new life… and new potency.

CRUSHING CREATES POTENCY

Crushing leads to a glorious outcome! While grapes are sweet and pleasant, they have little potency until they are crushed and finish the fermentation process. What was once sweet and pleasant turns potent. This is what I wanted in my life, in my parenting, in my speaking, in my prayer time, and in every other area of my life: Potency!

BEING A SWEET PERSON ISN'T WHAT MADE JESUS THE MOST FOLLOWABLE, POWERFUL, AND INFLUENTIAL PERSON IN HISTORY! IT WAS HIS POTENCY!

If our highest aim as a Christian is to be "sweet and pleasant" we're going to miss out on the abundant life that Jesus died for us to live. He said we would do greater works than he did (John 14:12)!

Jesus certainly was sweet and pleasant for the most part, but this wasn't his aim. His aim was to do the will of the Father and to be completely dead to himself so that he could bring heaven to the earth. Bringing heaven to earth takes a lot more than being a nice person. You have to be potent with the presence of God within!

Being a sweet person isn't what made Jesus the most followable, powerful, and influential person in history! It was his potency! With one touch, people were healed. With one word, people were delivered from demons. With one statement, he stunned the most intelligent leaders of his day. Jesus was potent and he died so that you and I could walk in that same potency.

The crushing comes before the catapult. Endure the crushing and surrender to the dying, then watch how life flows from you in potent and supernatural power. It's worth it.

Throughout this book, you will be given opportunities to walk through some crushing. You can read the words and intellectually grab the content, saying, "Oh, that's nice;" *or*, you can read the invitation to die in many areas and tell your heart, "Let's do this." If you choose the latter, you will become more and more potent in multiple areas of your life.

Don't just settle for "grape living." You were meant for more than just to be sweet and pleasant. You were made to be potent. Let's begin.

YOUR TURN TO RELEASE THE LOSSES

This is the first area of crushing we will walk through. It's a big one and it has the potential to release a wellspring of life on the inside of you that cannot be put into words. The joy in your heart and the lightness of your soul will be evident to you and everyone around you.

THE CRUSHING COMES BEFORE THE CATAPULT.

One thing that is really important to understand is that forgiving and releasing pain is a choice. The deeper the pain, the more committed you will need to be to this process we are going to walk through together. It's easier to just stuff it away and move on…. but *is it*? Stuffing it away leads to other pains, both physically and emotionally.

We are about to walk through an exercise together where you will be given an opportunity to release your own losses. Use the QR code below if you'd like to close your eyes, get comfortable, and listen to my voice. The other option is to continue reading the words below (which are similar to the recording). Either option works. Choose the one that allows you to be the most receptive. You may even decide to do both!

I want you to imagine something with me. Imagine that you are approaching the giant double doors of the throne room of God. Go ahead, push on the door and walk in. You see Father God sitting there on his beautiful throne waiting for you. He has a loving, kind, and gentle look in his eyes.

As you approach him, imagine that a bookshelf is sitting next to him. You notice that there are books on the shelf that are familiar to you. Pull one book from the shelf and look at it.

You realize this book is a painful story in your life. In fact, this shelf is holding the books of the stories of your life where the endings didn't quite turn out the way you wanted them to. Like the credits that roll at the end of a movie much too soon, this story you are holding ends in a way that has disappointed you. Maybe it's a loss of relationship with your sister. Maybe it's the loss of a child or parent. Maybe it's a loss of a career. When you hold this book, you realize that it has pain attached to it. There are no more blank pages in the back to write in a happy ending. The book just ended with pain. It is a book of loss.

Hold that book in your hands and read the cover. What is the title of the book? Allow yourself to begin to pull that pain up to the surface. Tell the Lord *aloud* why this book carries disappointment or pain. Say it from your heart, from your inner being. Allow yourself to feel this. Don't hold back from telling God the truth of how you feel. He already knows anyway. Take a moment to close your eyes and do this.

Now, when you are ready, hand the book to the Lord. Give him this loss. Really give it to him. Give him the judgment and pain that you've held against anyone involved in this story. Forgive them and let them free from your heart. Stop and do this before moving on.

Are there more books on the shelf that you need to repeat this with? Take the time to do that now.

Once you have given the Lord as many losses as you have awareness of, look in his eyes. See his compassion and love for you. Notice what he did with your books. Make a decision in your heart not to let the enemy or your memory haunt you with those books any longer. They are not yours anymore. They are not your possession. They belong to him now. Pause right here and make it a point to completely sever these losses from your heart.

Close your eyes now and see the Father's face. Allow his love and approval to fill you up. His Spirit is being poured out over you and in you. This is important that you allow his presence, his love for you, to overtake you. Make space in your heart to receive his love and find yourself giving your affection back to him. Pause to do this before moving on.

Next, you see him hand you a big, beautiful book with golden laced edges. The cover has your name on the front in big, bold font with the subtitle, *The Story of Your Beautiful Life*.

You open up the book and feel the texture of the thick paper. The illustrations contain colorful pictures of your family, your battles, your joys, your dreams, and many adventures. It is a collection of your incredible life. But as you flip through the pages, you notice that there are chapters that you have yet to live. You catch glimpses of art and words that you haven't yet experienced and a sense of adventure, hope, and provision washes over you. You flip to the back of the book in a hurry to see how this story ends and notice the last page has a picture of you sitting on your heavenly Father's lap, leaning back onto his chest. You are comfortable, anchored, and restful. **You are his.**

The words on the last page read, *Together, We Lived Happily Ever After.*

What did you experience during this time?

Record it here:

_____

_____

HE ISN'T DONE WITH YOUR STORY!

This was a special time with you and the Lord. He wants you to know that you are never ever alone - ever! He isn't done with your story!

WE MUST DIE IN ORDER TO HAVE TRUE LIFE!

3

THE DEATH - LIFE PARADOX

Before we dive into more stories of my crushing, which become invitations for your crushing, I want to make this clear: the Lord did not create hardship and throw it at me to see if I could endure it. He is not the author of destruction. Destruction is the work of Satan.

Jesus said these words:

> "A thief has only one thing in mind—he wants to steal, slaughter, and destroy. But I have come to give you everything in abundance, more than you expect —life in its fullness until you overflow!"
>
> John 10:10 TPT

This crushing process is not about Satan having a glory

moment over us! It's not about God giving us some sort of cosmic spanking in order to change us. Not at all! This is not the God we serve.

THE LORD DID NOT CREATE HARDSHIP AND THROW IT AT ME TO SEE IF I COULD ENDURE IT. HE IS NOT THE AUTHOR OF DESTRUCTION. DESTRUCTION IS THE WORK OF SATAN.

The crushing process works like a wrecking ball, tearing down all things that *don't* produce life within us: pride, fear, people-pleasing, performance, lying, addictions, toxic relationships, and much more.

In the case that Satan destroys something with Godly value, God will build it back even better, in abundance and even more than you expect! He will give life in its fullness *until you overflow!*

Tuck this in your heart! Digest it down into your soul! God is a good God and his plans for you and for me are only what we read here in John 10:10.

UNDERSTANDING THE DEATH - LIFE PARADOX

When I say, "wake up dead," this is instruction for how we can approach our life from our first waking moment of each day. We can be completely **awake** and **charged** with the power of the Holy Spirit, if - *and only if* - we will die to what our flesh wants. There is a competition going on:

FLESH = what Jenny wants
SPIRIT = what God wants

When the flesh *demands* for what it wants, it can snuff out the Spirit very easily. This fleshly desire can be anything from pride, to manipulation, to control, to temper tantrums, to laziness.

When we refuse to let our flesh have what it wants, we can say we are a "dead person."

The paradox here is that, when we're "dead," we are actually **fully alive** because the Spirit of God has permission and *space* to get in the driver's seat of our lives.

> Those who are **motivated by the flesh** only pursue *what benefits themselves*. But those who **live by the impulses of the Holy Spirit** are motivated to *pursue spiritual realities*.
>
> Romans 8:5 TPT (emphasis added)

Without the flesh driving the car of our lives, the Spirit is now able to drive. In this position, we begin to *think, act, and respond to the Holy Spirit's impulses, not the impulses of the flesh.* I guarantee that a day of being dead to the flesh is the best day you'll ever have because it is a day spent being led and impulsed by the Holy Spirit!

I GUARANTEE THAT A DAY OF BEING DEAD TO THE FLESH IS THE BEST DAY YOU'LL EVER HAVE BECAUSE IT IS A DAY SPENT BEING LED AND IMPULSED BY THE HOLY SPIRIT!

Look at what the Holy Spirit produces in us when we are impulsed by him instead:

> But the fruit produced by the Holy Spirit within you is **divine love** in all its varied expressions: **joy** that overflows, **peace** that subdues, **patience** that endures, **kindness** in action, a life full of **virtue**, **faith** that prevails, **gentleness** of heart, and **strength** of spirit. Never set the law above these qualities, for they are meant to be limitless.
>
> Galatians 5:22-23 TPT (emphasis added)

As we become mature followers of Christ, we will choose to be dead to our flesh so that the Holy Spirit can provide us with these wonderful attributes and live life to the fullest! Read the **bold words** in Galatians 5 again! Who wouldn't want these attributes operating within them every single day?

The condition here is that we must choose to be dead to our own desires and desire the things of God! We must die in order to have true life!

FROM THIS POINT FORWARD

I am going to spend a few more chapters teaching you about the hope-filled revelation I have about waking up dead and what the Bible says about living a dead life.

In part two, I'm going to share many of my own personal experiences of dying in certain aspects. These stories are true accounts and revelations that came from my own dying journey for you to glean from. I invite you to die right along with me. After all, potency and life to the fullest is your reward!

In the final portion of this book, I will share with you how to access Christ's power within your laid-down life in order to rise up in victory over your spiritual enemy. As a dead person, you are not passive. You need to know how to wage war over the one who wants to kill, steal, and destroy you.

I am positive that, even though I have come a long way, there are more places I will need to die after this book is in print. As my poem at the beginning of this book reflects, I don't live completely free from the struggle between the flesh and the Spirit. I am desperate for Christ to help me on a daily basis.

I'm comfortable with the process of growing and becoming more like Christ everyday. I have a vision of me at ninety-seven years old saying, "Wow, I can't believe how far I've come since ninety six!" Is there really such a thing as arriving? That would be neat, but while we're on this side of heaven, I believe that we will need to focus each and every day on this intentional decision to die to our selfish desires so that the Holy Spirit can cause us to be **fully alive!**

PERHAPS DYING TO SELF IS AS SIMPLE AS LETTING GO OF WHAT IS ALREADY DEAD AND GRABBING HOLD OF CHRIST WITHIN.

4

WEEKEND AT BERNIE'S

To get the *Wake Up Dead* revelation deep inside of us, let's get curious about a few places where the Bible talks about being "dead."

In my years of wanting to grow in God, I have learned that he loves to take us on a journey of discovery. If you know anything about life coaching, the very best coaches won't give you the answers. They will help you *discover* them! The Holy Spirit is the best coach there is, so his answers tend to be delivered in a way that requires us to lean into him as a friend. I call this discovery process "chasing breadcrumbs."

When we become curious about an area of growth in God, he will drop a crumb that hints towards what we're after. We have the choice to pick up that crumb and be curious about what God might be revealing. We can ask questions, lean into his heart through conversation, and uncover treasures in his word. One crumb after the next, he'll encourage us into an adventure of noticing, pondering, questioning, and discovering with him. It is one of the most profound ways to get to know him and ourselves. This journey will eventually lead to "the loaf of bread" where a life-giving revelation is waiting for us. Brilliant!

LET THE BREADCRUMBS FALL

My first curiosity in this dying journey was wondering what "dying to self" really means, especially since I am a Christian.

When someone gives their life to Christ, the Bible is very clear that our old identity has been crucified with Christ. We are emptied of our old self and Christ pours his life into us.

> **My old identity has been co-crucified with Messiah and no longer lives**; for the nails of his cross crucified me with him. And now the essence of this new life is no longer mine, for the Anointed One lives his life through me—we live in union as one! My new life is empowered by the faith of the Son of God who loves me so much that he gave himself for me, and dispenses his life into mine!
>
> Galatians 2:20 TPT (emphasis added)

According to this scripture, my old self is already dead. So, how can a Christian still need to "die" in some areas of our lives if we are already dead?

"Lord, help me with this one."

The scene of an old movie, *Weekend at Bernie's*, flashed in my mind. This is a breadcrumb!

Weekend at Bernie's is a 1989 American comedy film where two young insurance employees discover that their boss, Bernie, is dead. Caught in the middle of a scandal, these two men attempt to hide Bernie's death by propping his dead body up everywhere they go, incorporating him into everyday life. From water skiing to dancing, Bernie appears to be alive. Everywhere these men go, so does Bernie.

Instead of allowing Bernie to be dead and delivering him to the funeral home, they carry his heavy, dead, stinky body everywhere they go. They spend a ton of energy and effort making sure that Bernie participates in every living thing, even though he is totally dead.

After pondering this image of dragging around a dead body, I began to see what the Lord was revealing. Even though our old man dies when we receive Christ, we can pack this old identity around and prop it up at the family dinner table, drag it to work with us, and carry it into conversations with our spouse. We can even bring our dead man into chatter with ourselves and let it tell us how rotten we are.

BERNIE IN THE LABOR ROOM

In preparation for my childbirth without medication, the Holy Spirit told me I would need to let go of other people's experience and emotions. For instance, if my husband was not "doing what I wanted him to do," I would need to let that go. Holy Spirit said it would mess me up if I tried to control others or tend to other people's expectations of me.

Throughout my labor, I was focused on breathing in the presence of God so deeply, allowing the contractions to overtake my body (rather than trying to run away from them). This was working so well from contraction to contraction until all of a sudden, I had this random thought: *I hope my mom isn't disappointed that I didn't ask her to be in here with me.*

Whoa! My uterus pinched down and stabbing pain gripped my entire lower body. It was unbearable. I knew instantly that this one little thought of "feeling guilty" had caused my pain to shoot through the roof. FEAR had increased the pain!

Bernie showed up in the labor room and tried to tell me that I should feel bad for my mom and guilty for not creating a better experience for her. The reality was, my mom didn't care. I didn't care. But my old identity (old, fleshy, icky Bernie) wanted to do one thing: CONTROL how others feel about me.

As soon as the pain surged into my body, I dropped the guilty thought! I was back on track in my true identity — focusing on the presence of the Holy Spirit — receiving the tangible inhale and exhale of the love of God. It only took a nanosecond for me to switch my mind over from fear to love and the pain immediately subsided.

BERNIE'S DEAD TO ME

Have you ever said something to someone you love so much that had no life in it at all? Have you ever thought something that came from a place of fear and control? If you're human, the answer is *yes*. We've all said and thought stinky stuff that hurt ourselves and other people. Was that Bernie talking?

If our old identity is dead but we continue to bring it with us everywhere we go, it's like hauling around stinky, heavy, rotten Bernie. When we feel something stinky rise up in our hearts, we must realize there is something dead trying to participate in our new life. This creates *mixture*.

Mixture is when our new life and our old life try to share the same space. It's similar to spraying beautiful perfume over dog poop on the carpet. We don't want to be people of mixture.

For instance, we don't want to express love while also giving off vibes of stress, gossip, control, manipulation, anger, bitterness, etc. You and I both know that being around a person like this is confusing and unpleasant. Even if there are sniffs of love drafting out of the stink, you still just want to get away from them!

WHEN WE FEEL SOMETHING STINKY RISE UP IN OUR HEARTS, WE MUST REALIZE THERE IS SOMETHING DEAD TRYING TO PARTICIPATE IN OUR NEW LIFE.

So, what should we do when our old, dead identity tries to come and stink up our new life? We certainly don't want to be the person we just described above! The scriptures say that we must join and become one with the Holy Spirit, seeing our old flesh nature as dead and unresponsive.

What if, when we felt control or anger begin to rise up in us, we simply didn't respond? Like someone knocking at your door, are you really obligated to open it and let them in?

> …Since you are now joined with him, **you must continually view yourselves as dead and unresponsive to sin's appeal while living daily for God's pleasure in union with Jesus**, the Anointed One.
>
> Romans 6:11b TPT (emphasis added)

What I see here is that *we must continually view ourselves as dead and unresponsive to sin's appeal* while deep diving into union with Jesus.

Perhaps dying to self is as simple as letting go of what is already dead and grabbing hold of Christ within.

FIRST LOVE

Before we move forward, let's explore this very real challenge: How do we grab ahold of Christ within?

The answer is, we allow ourselves to fall in love. You see, what we love, we cling to. What we cling to, we aren't willing to let go of.

The truth is, I can tell you until I'm blue in the face that it's a really good thing to "die to your own life," but whether or not you will *do* it will come down to who (or what) your First Love is.

> **IF WE LOVE OUR OWN LIVES FIRST AND TRY TO LOVE GOD SECOND, WE SETTLE FOR A "MIXTURE" AND END UP ACHING FOR SO MUCH MORE.**

If we love our own lives first and try to love God second, we settle for a "mixture" and end up aching for so much more. Once you taste and see that the Lord is good and experience his tangible presence, you'll never want to forfeit it for a cheap and temporary one-night-stand with the world.

> Drink deeply (taste and see) of the pleasures of this God. Experience for yourself the joyous mercies he gives to all who turn to hide themselves in him.
>
> Psalm 34:8 TPT

To taste and see the goodness and love of God requires building a foundation with Christ based on knowing each other deeply. At our ministry events, we call this kind of intimacy: "IN-TO-ME-SEE." Intimacy is formed wherever we allow ourselves to be known, seen, vulnerable, and open - flaws and all. Intimacy with God is about allowing God to see you and you to see him.

The world would like to narrow the meaning of intimacy down

to sexual behavior and pervert what God intended intimacy to be. Intimacy can't be narrowed down to sexual behavior. Intimacy is about fulfilling our greatest need as human beings: to be known.

When we open up our hearts to God's love, his counsel, his presence, his power, his care, his correction, and his blessings, we become more than church-goers. We become daughters and sons who know him. He is literally with you right now, closer than your breath, interested in every single detail of your life. He is caring for you in ways that only he knows are right for your unique imprint. He's cleaning wounds that you may settle with or may not even realize you have. He's been in your future, forming plans for good and not for harm (see Jeremiah 29:11) and he's been to your past to cleanse all of your sin.

When we have experienced the first love of the Father, we will be willing to "die to our own life" and grab ahold of Christ. He is extremely interested and invested in you. He is patient with you and committed to your journey. He walks hand in hand with you. As you allow yourself to let go of loving your own life and instead, cling to Christ, he will fill you with deep satisfaction of every kind to overflowing!

CHOOSING LIFE WILL REQUIRE DEATH.

5

DEAD MAN TALKING

At this point in our journey, I am going to help you absorb and digest what you've ingested so far. Let's walk through this content with a few exercises to help you get this in your spirit.

"I'm not good enough."

> **That's dead.** Christ within me can conquer every difficulty.
> (Philippians 4:13)

"I'm so ashamed."

> **That's dead.** Christ within me took all the punishment

for my sin on himself.
(Romans 3:21-26)

"I can't believe he said that."

That's dead. Christ within me forgave and forgot the hateful things that I've also said.
(Romans 3:24)

"We'll never get ahead."

That's dead. Christ within me has every resource I need.
(Matthew 6:31-32)

"I'm better than her."

That's dead. Christ within me is Supreme over all.
(Colossians 1:17-18)

"I'm not spiritual enough for God to love me."

That's dead. Christ within proved he loved me when he died for me.
(John 3:16)

"This is too hard. I can't do this."

That's dead. Christ within is made strongest when I am weak.
(2 Corinthians 12:9)

Has your dead man been talking? From now on, every time you hear your dead man talk, you can respond aloud, "That's dead." Then follow it up with a truth about Christ who has poured himself and all he is inside of you.

To find a truth, go to your search engine. Type in the statement that fits how you feel and then add the word "scripture" at the end. For example, you would type:

Feeling lonely scripture

You will get multiple pages telling you where in the Bible to find scriptures that you can use as the truth to combat the lie. After you write it, say it aloud three times with authority! (See Appendix on page 241 for easy reference.)

YOUR TURN

Let's practice seeing ourselves as dead and unresponsive to sin.

What is the most recent and ridiculous accusation your dead man has said to you?

_____

_____

Now, it's simple. Say aloud, "That's dead." Pause and ask the Holy Spirit, *"What is the truth?"* Next, search up a scripture that will edify the truth.

Write it here:

_____

_____

_____

Finally, say this scripture aloud three times with authority!

A FORK IN THE ROAD

I was sitting with my thirteen-year-old daughter and her two friends as they were having an argument. One of the little girls felt that she was being left out and feelings had been hurt. How familiar it is to begin to feel insecure, rejected, and unloved as a girl at this age!

I gave them the picture of a fork in the road. A sign sat at the fork giving them the option to take the road of "I am unloved. I am not good enough. I am not important;" *or*, they could head down the road of "I am loved. God loves me. God delights in me. I have love in me that I want to give to my friends today."

I told them that they would stand at this fork in the road multiple times a day. The most wonderful part was that they would get to *choose* which road to travel!

> "… I have set before you life and death, blessings and curses. Now choose life, so that you and your children may live."
>
> Deuteronomy 30:19b NIV

Remember the "choose your own adventure" books where you had the choice at the end of the chapter to turn to a specific page if you wanted the main character to go in one direction, or another page for a different course of action? This is what we have to do dozens of times a day: decide which of the two roads to take. Every time we feel a negative pull, mindset, or attitude, we have to stand at the fork in the road and see that one is labeled "selfishness" and the other "love." We all stand here multiple times a day, but do we stop and realize that we have a choice?

One must be warned: the one you choose is the one you will experience for the rest of the day, and if chosen repetitively, you will experience it for a lifetime.

After praying the dangerous prayer in 2019, my husband and

I lost a twenty-year business (I will share this story in detail in another chapter). When we received the phone call that we were going to lose everything, we were left standing at the fork in the road. Bob and Jenny got to choose our own adventure, starting with our thoughts. The enemy held up a sign that said, *You'll never recover. You should be very afraid. Let's talk about all the scary things that will happen to you and your family.* Meanwhile, the Holy Spirit was standing with calm authority, inviting us to follow Him. He simply said, *"Be still. This is the beginning of a new season of your life. I'll take care of you. Follow Me."*

Let's reflect on this and drive it home. Close your eyes and envision yourself at a fork in the road. The *accusation* of the dead man that you identified earlier is labeled on one road and the *truth* that the Holy Spirit gave you is labeled on the other road.

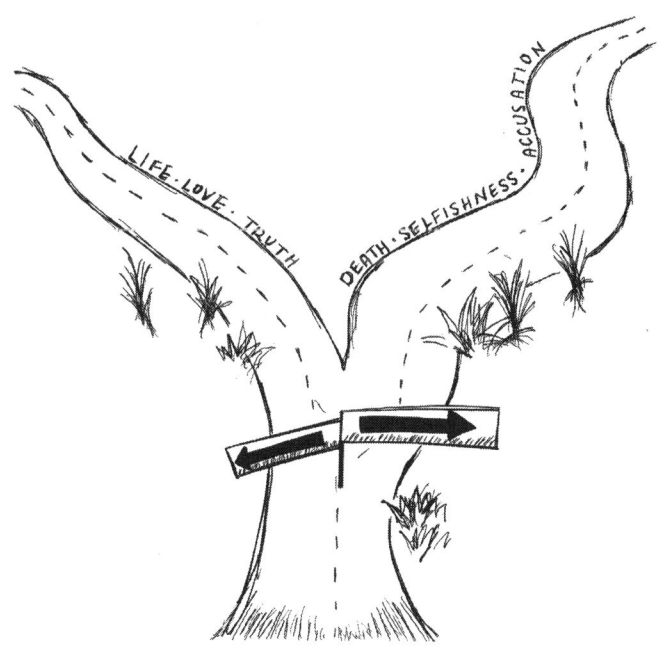

He has set before you life and death. Now, choose the one you want to experience. Use the QR CODE for a short audio exercise with me… or keep reading!

Go ahead, close your eyes and take a step down the road of accusation (death) or the road of truth (life). What do you sense? What do you feel? Do you feel more free; more love; more joy and generosity? Do you feel relieved, energized, and empowered? What does it feel like to take the road of accusation and selfishness? Write what you are experiencing to the side of the road that you chose. This is a quick journaling exercise to help lock in the feelings that you can look forward to by choosing life.

RECOGNIZING THE DEAD MAN

So often, we follow that false identity down the road to death without even giving it one thought that we are choosing to drag our dead man around. In order to become totally new people, filled with new life, we must begin to take note of where we have failed to realize what is dead, and then submit to the burial of our old identity.

How will we know if we haven't submitted to this burial? How will we know if our dead man is still talking? Our mindset will stink! Our emotions will feel heavy! It will feel like we're dragging dead weight around in our hearts and minds. Our dead man will not give life to others at all, it will only create more death in and around us. We will find it harder and harder to encourage others and feel hopeful in life.

What if being dead to ourselves is as simple as seeing dead things as dead and decide to be unresponsive to the sin that tries to lure our response?

Simple? Yes. Easy? Definitely not. Choosing life will require death.

DEATH BRINGS FORTH LIFE

If you have received Jesus Christ into your heart, you died with him! Your old man is now dead, but look at what happens after we are buried with Christ:

> Sharing in his death by our baptism means that we were **co-buried and entombed with him**, so that when the Father's glory raised Christ from the dead, **we were also raised with him**. We have been co-resurrected with him so that we could be **empowered to walk in the freshness of new life**. For since we are permanently grafted into him to experience a death like his, then we are permanently grafted into him to experience a resurrection like his and the new life that it imparts.
> Romans 6:4-5 TPT (emphasis added)

In order to let the fresh new life spring up inside of us, we have to allow our old identity to be buried! We can't have a resurrected new life without the burial. We follow the same pattern of Christ who died and then resurrected life followed.

When we let our old identity die, we make room for Christ to come in with his identity.

Old Identity (self is god)	**New Life (God is God)**
Control	Trust
Anger	Joy
My Way	His Way
Fear	Love
Greed	Generosity

Old Identity	New Life
Jealousy	Encouragement
Disorder	Order
Depression	Gladness
Addictions	Intimacy with God
Never Good Enough	Lacking nothing
Critical	Unconditional Love
Agitated	Gentle
Passive	Active

This list could go on for a hundred pages, but you get the point. Our old identity is marked by self with eyes turned inward to control and protect, but a new life of love and service springs forward when we die to ourselves.

What are some of the dead things from your old identity that you would like to see buried in exchange for new life? List those dead things below on the left (attitudes, negative mindsets, addictions, relational tensions, etc.). Know that God delights in our transparency with him!

Now, ask him what new life you can expect to spring forth from each of these items once you agree that those old things have no place and no authority in your life. Simply agree to let Bernie die right here. Record the new thing that will spring to life in the right column.

I've already prayed that he will see your words here and begin the process of burying the old, dead parts and resurrecting new life within!

Old Identity (self is god)   New Life (God is God)

_____   _____

_____   _____

_____   _____

Lord, help me choose life and not death!

A SEED CARRIES A DESTINY CODE TO BECOME SOMETHING AND FULFILL A PURPOSE.

6

DIE TO MULTIPLY

We have a drive-through restaurant in town that includes a packet of seeds with their kids meals. The idea of planting some tomatoes or onions is very endearing, but I never do. I lovingly shove them in our junk drawer and let them believe that someday, I will plant them and see them come into their full destiny.

Even though these tomato seeds have the potential to produce tomatoes for days, I've yet to open the drawer and witness a single tomato spring to life. Nope, that packet just sits there doing absolutely nothing.

You and I both know that those seeds can stay in the packet for a thousand years and we still won't get a single tomato. Why is that? Potential will stay in a state of potential until it is interrupted and activated.

DYING TO BECOME MORE

A seed carries a destiny code to become something and fulfill a purpose. To be activated, it must come under pressure and darkness until the outer shell breaks open. The outer layer dies away, allowing the inside elements to take nutrition and moisture from the soil. The beginnings of what will become a tomato can now wiggle its way to the surface and into existence.

POTENTIAL WILL STAY IN A STATE OF POTENTIAL UNTIL IT IS INTERRUPTED AND ACTIVATED.

Jesus was a seed with a destiny code on the inside of him. His code was written from the beginning of time: die a death humanity should have died and crush the head of Satan. If he didn't obey the Father's instruction to give up his life and die, he wouldn't have defeated Satan for us.

Jesus shared this analogy to describe why he had to die:

> "Let me make this clear: A single grain of wheat will never be more than a single grain of wheat unless it drops into the ground and dies. Because then it sprouts and produces a great harvest of wheat—all because one grain died."
>
> John 12:24 TPT

At the time, there was only one human Jesus. He was using the analogy of a grain of wheat to help his disciples understand that he wasn't going away to leave them, but to leave as one person and come back multiplied and alive.

How did Jesus multiply? He came back as the Holy Spirit who is *everywhere*. The Holy Spirit is with you right now. He is "Jesus everywhere." He is with your friends and family right now. Before his death and resurrection, Jesus was one man in one place. He wasn't omnipresent. He knew that his one life would be buried and then the Holy Spirit would be released from him all throughout the earth, multiplied!

Like Jesus, you have a destiny code written on the inside of you! You and I have the potential for immeasurable, multiplied life to come out of us: overflowing joy, overwhelming peace, abundant generosity, extravagant kindness, and so much more. Each of us has a destiny code inside of us that has instructions to fulfill a specific purpose. However, unless we let our selfish outer shell die, we won't see that purpose accomplished in our lives.

Clinging to our old outer shell might look like protecting our comforts; holding on to what is safe and familiar; clinging to our opinions; becoming our own god; loving money; loving position and power; or cooperating with the world's view of right and wrong. We can refuse to come out of our junk-drawer life and stay tucked away safely in our packet of self preservation.

THAT PRETTY PICTURE ISN'T SO PRETTY

Social media is full of pictures that only appear on the outside of a person's seed packet. We post pictures of our smiling families, laughing kids, and perfectly neat houses. Only *we* know if those pictures are truly what is bursting forth from the inside of us.

Christ died so that we could have *actual* life bursting from within whether we're posting about it on social media or not. We can all smile on the outside for a picture (and I hope you do), but what about the nighttime giggles, sincere apologies, and overflowing kindness between you and your spouse? What about the forgiveness for an offense, courageous exploits for Jesus, and the loving correction to a child that no one will ever experience but you?

The reality for us all is that we were born with a stubborn, dead, prideful outer shell that really wants to clam up and hang on. This is where the rubber meets the road. Will we die so that he can live through us?

Some of us have the idea that Jesus will just bust out of us from the inside, bypassing our will and throwing our old, dead identity out of his way. In reality, we are given free will to choose this day whom we will serve: the selfish nature within us that desires to be our own god, or Christ.

After we invite Jesus to be Lord of our lives, he sits on a throne in our hearts and *waits* for a crack in our outer shell where he can dispense his Spirit out of us. Our part is to let go, let go, and let go some more. This is when Christ can burst forth with light and love from within!

Are you exhausted from dragging dead Bernie around? Let go. Are you so done with your selfishness, pride, and stinky attitude? Let go. You can decide they don't have a place in your life anymore and allow Christ to rule within your mind and heart. As you let go, let go, and let go again, your old shell will break and over time, vanish, and Christ will come bursting through.

THE ONLY WAY TO DESTINY IS DEATH

Some of us want to sit inside our life packet holding out for the picture of what we might become someday without having to face the reality that a death and burial is the only way there.

I distinctly remember the day I sat in the spa dressing room with my friend, Pastor Callie, and cried tears of frustration. God was calling me out of my safe package of private ministry and into public ministry. My heart was being stretched towards hosting conferences and horrific thoughts of speaking LIVE on Facebook.

A DEATH AND BURIAL IS THE ONLY WAY THERE.

I was totally freaked out and I didn't want to endure the persecution I knew deep down would come from this decision. We were involved in a business at that time and there were already rumblings of people expressing their disapproval of me sharing

Jesus openly.

I wanted to do this from inside my packet where I was safe from mean people and too much attention. I knew that going public with the gospel and my testimony would cause judgment, criticism, and probably loss in different forms. I also knew that it would place a focus on me that I was uncomfortable with.

There would be a price to pay and I would have to die to many, many counterfeit comforts and insecurities. I just sat in my spa robe and tearfully whimpered, "Callie, I don't want this to be about me. I don't want people's eyes on me."

> **THERE WOULD BE A PRICE TO PAY AND I WOULD HAVE TO DIE TO MANY, MANY COUNTERFEIT COMFORTS AND INSECURITIES.**

Her answer was one that I knew was true: "Jenny, this is about you answering the call on your life." It was just that simple.

After a good cry and honest confession that day, I realized the only way for this calling to pour out of me would be the same way a seed breaks forth its destiny: I would have to bury that intimidated, frightened, concerned, insecure old identity. Just. Let. It. Go.

Some of us are sitting inside our safe packet and praying that God will turn us into the picture on the front without a death and a burial of our old selves. Ultimately, we are just like a seed. We will only see Christ burst out of us when we allow ourselves to be buried under pressure and darkness.

Sounds like a good time, right?

But really, you want to read this next scripture because this death, burial, rise-to-new-life process is what Jesus said would actually lead us into our most fulfilling life:

> "The person who loves his life and pampers himself will miss true life! But the one who detaches his life from this world and abandons himself to me, will find true

life and enjoy it forever! If you want to be my disciple, follow me and you will go where I am going. And if you truly follow me as my disciple, the Father will shower his favor upon your life."

John 12:25 TPT

As scary as it sounds to a*bandon ourselves to him*, look what we receive on the other side! This scripture says we will find true life and enjoy it forever! The Father will shower his favor upon us! Living in true life is much better than living in the *idea* of true life.

WHAT "COULD BE" NEVER "WILL BE" UNLESS WE DIE

From here, I invite you to die and be buried with Christ, because the life that springs forth from Christ within is AWESOME!

You might wonder at this point which areas of life you need to let die and be buried. I believe the Lord may have the same breadcrumb-chasing answer for you that he had for me:

"You'll see."

DYING

HAS ITS

REWARDS!

7

DYING "QUICK REFERENCE"

To get this burial party started, I've made a list of ten major places where I've personally experienced the heaviest degree of loss, burying, and crushing, and consequently, the most growth. These are ten places in life we may have in common. Most of us will come to a fork in the road in these areas and we'll get to choose whether to cling to our life or let it go and cling to God instead.

Read each of these areas and do a heart check. Ask the Holy Spirit to reveal to you which of these you are dealing with in this season. If you find any of these areas poking or pulling at you from the inside, pray the prayer or declaration following that specific section aloud. Remember that LIFE is on the other side of death!

THE TEN R'S

1. RELATIONSHIPS

"Jesus had a Judas." The first time I experienced outright betrayal by a person I thought was my forever friend, the Holy Spirit spoke these words to me. Judas was the disciple who turned Jesus into the authorities, which led to his crucifixion. If Jesus was betrayed and he was perfect, we will also be betrayed. In Mark 14, we read about Jesus being betrayed by all of the disciples when he went to the Garden of Gethsemane to pray. He asked them to stay up and pray for him during the most terrifying moment of his life and returned to find them all asleep. If you can relate to this betrayal or disappointment, I want to invite you to let it go. Would you pray this prayer with me?

> **IF JESUS WAS BETRAYED AND HE WAS PERFECT, WE WILL ALSO BE BETRAYED.**

Lord, I forgive everyone who has betrayed me or fallen asleep when I needed them the most. Thank you, God, that you have never left me and never will. I ask you to bring God-centered relationships into my life that will bring LIFE to me. I pray this in Jesus' name, amen.

2. RECLUSIVENESS

Do you ever struggle with wanting to be around people and sharing your life with them? Maybe you prefer to avoid the risk and messiness of relationships. Maybe you were betrayed and have decided that you can't trust very many people. This may be an area that the Lord is going to invite you to die in.

In late 2019, I had a vision of the enemy grabbing the horizontal wooden bar of a cross. He was mumbling, *"Fine. You can have your oneness with God, but I'm taking your oneness with people."*

The vertical post of the cross represented our intimacy with Christ and the horizontal bar represented intimacy with others. It was as if the enemy was trying to dismantle the power of the cross by disconnecting us from one another.

I didn't understand why I was seeing this until the COVID-19 pandemic hit a few months later! We all saw how the enemy worked overtime to separate us from each other for a very long time (as I'm writing this, we are still in the throws of this strategy). The enemy knows that if he can isolate and separate us from the body of Christ, he can deceive us more easily. Our brothers and sisters in Christ who are standing with their shields beside us and behind us are no longer there and now the enemy can get to us from behind. If this sounds familiar, I invite you to pray the following prayer with me.

Lord, you said in Genesis 2:18 that it is not good for man to be alone. You made me to be deeply connected to people who I call 'family.' I am asking you to forgive me for isolating myself or being selfish with my time, energy and gifts. Give me the courage to share my life with others. In Jesus' name, amen.

3. RESOURCES

You cannot outgive God. No matter how much you give, you will always receive more. We don't give in order to get. We give because we are generous and show our worship to God by giving away something that is valuable to us. However, the kingdom principle stands true that you will never be the last one standing, showing God that you gave more than he was able to give to you.

I have so many stories of how God asked us to stretch our giving (until it stung a little). In that, we saw God miraculously pay off bills, come through with business growth that couldn't be explained logically, and show up supernaturally in times of desperation. When we heard about the kingdom principle of giving, we knew that we needed to get seed in the ground on a consistent basis. The Bible says a lot about giving, sowing seed, and reaping a harvest.

This is one of my favorite things that Jesus said about letting go of our resources and giving them away:

> "Give, and you will receive. Your gift will return to you in full—pressed down, shaken together to make room for more, running over, and poured into your lap. The amount you give will determine the amount you get back."
>
> Luke 6:38 NLT

Lord, show me where I need to plant my resources in good soil! Help me to trust your word that I am not depleted when I give, but running over! I thank you that you see my gift as pure as I give it cheerfully, from a place of worship. In Jesus' name, amen.

4. BEING "RIGHT"

There are times that we can be totally right and completely wrong at the same time. For instance, when I was first married and really didn't understand this, I would bring up a life issue in the evening with Bob. He would be laying in bed, so tired. I would ask a question and he would mumble something back at me or give me a one-word answer. His groans and mumbles turned to not caring about what I was saying and grabbing a blanket to go sleep on the couch.

I was offended because the subject matter was legitimate. I was "right" in needing to clear the matter, discuss a business issue or ask about how to solve a problem the next day. Not only was he not putting energy into the conversation, but he was now stonewalling me.

The fact was, the issue I was bringing up was legitimately "right." We needed to talk about it. But, my timing was wrong. So wrong.

One day I got an image of a person putting their hand on a hot stove, getting burned. Foolishly, they did it again, amazed that they got burned again. Then, they did it again!

Holy Spirit asked me right then, *"Have you noticed that every time you bring up a topic at night right before bed, you are both getting burned?"* That was the day I died to being RIGHT at NIGHT! I was under the illusion that because I was "right" about the subject we needed to talk about, I couldn't be in the wrong. The facts are, I discovered that the right thing at the wrong time is a mistake. This was the cause of the majority of our fights: improper timing. I had to die to that.

> **THERE ARE TIMES THAT WE CAN BE TOTALLY RIGHT AND COMPLETELY WRONG AT THE SAME TIME.**

It feels really good to be right, but does anybody like a know-it-all? If you need help dying in this area of "I'm always right," here is a prayer for you:

Lord, I hate being wrong. You know that. So, I'm going to need your help with this. I am sorry for being prideful enough to think I have to be right. I humble myself right now and ask you to give me an accurate glimpse of my own imperfections. Help me not to be discouraged when I see my flaws. Help me love well in my weaknesses by apologizing, not estimating myself as higher than I am, and serving others with gentleness and humility. In Jesus' name, amen.

5. RECOGNITION

"If you don't live by the praise of men you won't die by their criticism." Bill Johnson, Bethel Church, Redding California

IF WE ARE PUTTING OUR IDENTITY IN THE PRAISES OF MEN, WE WILL BEGIN TO PERFORM FOR THEM AND FEAR THEM.

As human beings, we love to take credit — for the good stuff. But, when it comes to failures, our flesh likes to deny it had anything to do with it and often goes one step further to find someone else to blame.

We love praise, and that's not all bad. I know that there is a deep need in us to be recognized for our efforts. I believe that this desire is rooted in the innate desire to be known.

However, being recognized can be a slippery slope. There are seasons you will go through that God won't let you take any credit or recognition because he wants that counterfeit identity to be squashed. If we are putting our identity in the praises of men, we will begin to perform for them and fear them.

I believe that God loves it when we assess ourselves accurately. When we see that something went well that we had our hand in, we can confidently and humbly say, "I loved being a part of that." But when we position ourselves and our language around being "the one" who people praise, we're off track.

Recently, my leadership team and I realized that some organizational systems weren't going so well. We got together to discuss how to change it. At first, we wanted to be frustrated that people weren't "getting it." After looking at it from all angles, we knew that as a leadership team, we hadn't properly outlined a strategy and expectations for people to follow. We realized we wanted people to read our minds. *We* were the reason it wasn't working. We were the ones who didn't execute it properly the first time, and we were also the ones with the power to implement a better strategy the next time!

Do you see how this works? You die to the thing you want to hang onto only to get POWER and LIFE in return. Dying has its rewards!

Lord, I give you the side of me that wants to be seen as perfect in the eyes of others. I sever myself from the deception that I need to be praised by others. I step boldly into a place of humility where I can celebrate the areas where I contributed well and recognize the areas where I did not contribute well. Because you know me and approve of me, I don't need to always be seen in a perfect light by others. In Jesus' name, amen.

6. REPUTATION

If we try to "put on" a certain look or image so that we can be known for something in order to gain popularity, we will constantly be striving to be someone we are not. This isn't true freedom. God told me something that may not seem very inspiring to you, but it comforted me greatly: *"Jenny, you are a needy nobody. You are needy for me and a nobody to the world."* I was so happy that I didn't have to build myself up to be a "somebody" to the world. He gave me permission to be a little girl, grabbing her daddy's pant leg. Needy. Fragile. Desperate for his presence twenty-four seven. As for the world? I didn't need to create someone for them to love or receive well.

He said that he has called me to do a certain work on the earth and to do it in complete neediness for him and in my true identity, not in the identity of the culture. After he shared this with me, I stumbled upon Paul referring to himself as an "unknown nobody" in 2 Corinthians 6:9.

Lord, I lay down the need to live in a perceived 'greater image.' I was made in your image, so I am already the true me right now. I love how you made me. I admit that I am totally needy for you, desperate actually. I don't have to build my reputation up to the world, I only need to give the world real love that comes from you. I don't need to be known by the world because I'm known by you. I declare this in Jesus' name, amen.

7. RELIGION

If I had to choose my favorite passage of the Bible, it would be Mary Magdalene, the prostitute, kissing Jesus' feet. This broken woman, who had seven demons cast out of her by Jesus, was finally free and couldn't stop lavishing him with love.

Here is the gist of the story: Jesus was having dinner at Simeon's house, a Jewish religious leader. Mary came through the door and fell at Jesus' feet, kissing them and wiping his feet with her tears. Simeon was disgusted with the fact that Jesus would let a prostitute kiss his feet and questioned in his heart if Jesus was truly a prophet. Simeon was a religious man who, in his own mind, had been made clean before God by *what he did for God*. This woman was overcome with gratitude for what Jesus *had done for her* and couldn't stop kissing his feet and even poured out her expensive perfume over him.

Jesus, knowing what Simeon was thinking in his heart, said to him,

> "… Do you see this woman kneeling here? She is doing for me what you didn't bother to do. When I entered your home as your guest, you didn't think about offering me water to wash the dust off my feet. Yet she came into your home and washed my feet with her many tears and then dried my feet with her hair. You didn't even welcome me into your home with the customary

kiss of greeting, but from the moment I came in she has not stopped kissing my feet. You didn't take the time to anoint my head with fragrant oil, but she anointed my head and feet with the finest perfume. She has been forgiven of all her many sins. This is why she has shown me such extravagant love. But those who assume they have very little to be forgiven will love me very little."

Luke 7:44-47 TPT

After this, Jesus forgave *all* of Mary's sins as she worshipped at his feet.

God will ask each one of us to die to the belief that our "good work" will get us clean before God. It is only because of Jesus' death and resurrection on the cross that we are able to be clean before God. I absolutely love this woman's devotion and abandonment to her reputation in order to be split open in gratitude before the King.

> **RELIGION IS THE BEHAVIOR, RITUALS, AND CHECK BOXES WE WANT TO LEAN ON TO MAKE OURSELVES FEEL ACCEPTED AND SUCCESSFUL IN GOD'S EYES.**

Religion is the behavior, rituals, and check boxes we want to lean on to make ourselves feel accepted and successful in God's eyes. It's actually when we die to religion and lean back on the Savior as our confidence that we will spring up in life and devotion. Leaning on religion leads us to arrogance or shame (if we can't uphold the perfection required). Leaning on Christ sets us free!

Lord, I leave my religious ideas of self-righteousness behind. I don't want any of it. I only want you. You are my Savior. You are my rescuer. I devote myself to you, not my doing. If you have found arrogance or self-righteousness in me rooted in religion, I command it to be severed off my life completely. I am like Mary Magdalene worshipping at your feet for what you did for me! I am forgiven of my many sins. In Jesus' name, amen."

8. REHEARSING THE PAST

The devil loves the rewind button! Sometimes people will suddenly have a wave of memories from the past because the devil doesn't have any new accusations against you! Be aware when your mind begins to rehearse a situation that upset you. Many times, this is a strategy of the enemy to drive unforgiveness and offense against someone deep into your heart. He knows if he can get you mad at others or yourself, you will get trapped in replaying the scene over and over again in your mind. You know what happens next? You can't move forward in creativity, inspiration, new relationships, new ideas, etc. You're now high-centered on an old issue.

So, what do we do if those old things pop up? You may need to repeat the exercise on forgiveness or losses written for you in this book. You may need to ask Jesus to come into that scene with you and take control of what happened. Watch what he does. You may notice that he changes the scenario altogether. You may notice that he wants you to apologize to someone. You may notice that he is going to flush the whole thing down the toilet. All I can tell you is that you cannot rehearse negative moments and expect to create new positive ones. THIS IS A TRAP AND YOU NEED TO LET IT GO.

If I have a hard time letting myself go for something I did that wasn't my best, I hear the Lord say to me, *"Jenny, was my cross enough, or do I need to be tortured some more?"* This question always brings me to the place where I can humble myself and let go of whatever is offending me or tormenting me. If I believe that the abuse and death my Lord endured for me was enough, then it needs to be enough! I have to, once again, agree with the power of his death and resurrection. This is where I just let it go. It's done. "Tetelestai." The last words spoken by Jesus before he gave up his Spirit.

Lord, I take hold and capture all of my past that wants to haunt or torment me and I lay it at the cross. I decree what Paul said in Philippians 3:13, 'I don't depend on my own strength to accomplish this; however I do have one compelling focus: I forget all of the past as I fasten my heart to the future instead.' I do not have the ability to reconcile these matters, but you do. You dealt with these things at the cross and I agree that your death on the cross was enough for all of my past, present, and future to be wiped clean. I plead the blood of Jesus over my past, my present, and my future. You are enough, God. What you did for me was enough. I let it go. In Jesus' name, amen.

9. REASONING

This one is sneaky. We love to understand things so that we can be in control. But this isn't the way of the kingdom. As believers, we are called to live, not by sight, but by FAITH (2 Corinthians 5:7).

> **I MADE UP MY MIND THAT I COULD NOT REASON WITH WHAT I SAW IN THE NATURAL.**

When I had my very first teenage girl and I didn't quite know how to parent the ups and downs of the hormone rollercoaster, I would find myself exhausted and discouraged at what I was witnessing with my eyes. For a family that has been nurturing our children in Christ from day one, I didn't understand how these challenges were hitting our child. I would try to fix her and help her and… well, control her, if I'm honest. She was the one who got me to pray on a consistent basis. All of my fixing and fidgeting over trying to REASON with her wasn't working. I couldn't do much of anything without making it worse.

Feeling totally defeated in prayer, I heard the Lord say, *"What you see in her behavior isn't real. That's all fake."* Okay, wait, I had to wrap my mind around this. He went on. *"Yes, you are seeing something that isn't real. Can I show you what is real?"* Suddenly, I saw an image of my daughter playing the piano and singing her heart out. So much joy and freedom was in this image and God assured me that this image in my mind was what was real.

My spirit caught it and I made up my mind that I could not REASON with what I saw in the natural. From that day forward, he told me to pray for her and parent her as if she was living that out right now. My prayers changed from *ugh* prayers to *"Thank you, God, that you have put a song in her heart, joy out of her mouth, and a voice for the nations!"*

It took several months of prayer from that place of faith, but she popped out of her "fake life" and entered her real life! She came to me one day and vaguely expressed the desire to have a keyboard. I put her in the car right away! We went to the music store and I bought the keyboard as fast as I could. We set it up in her room and that night, with her door shut, she played her keyboard and began to sing. She didn't know we could all hear her. I sat in the hallway against the wall and let the tears stream down my face. I could hear pure joy coming out of her for the first time in years. What was *real in heaven* had arrived on earth.

She spent the next few years on a worship team, most of the time from the keyboard. Her keyboard became her prayer portal and love language with the Father.

I am here to tell you, I couldn't have reasoned my way through this. It was an absolute mystery to me to why she was experiencing such turmoil and my reasoning wasn't going to save the day. The only thing I could do was die to reason and pick up the shield of faith in dedicated prayer. My anthem in those dark times became, *"I believe you, God."*

Lord, Proverbs 3:5 says I shouldn't lean on my own understanding, but submit all of my ways to you. You do things different than I do. I admit that I want to understand to control, but what I truly desire is to live in FAITH. I let go of what I want to understand and what I think I understand and pick up FAITH. Give me an image of my life that requires me to believe you and walk in great faith. I'm ready let go of what I see and believe you. In Jesus' name, amen.

10. REBELLION

Rebellion is where all of humanity got into a mess. Adam and Eve were doing really well until Eve did the opposite of what God instructed her to do. She was told she could eat from any tree in the garden of Eden except for one. He pointed out one little tree out of all of the trees and said, *"don't eat from this one."* Adam and Eve agreed, but it wasn't long before the serpent (Satan) tricked Eve into eating from the tree. Do you know how he tricked her? He simply told her that if she ate from the tree that she'd be "like" God. He pitched her the dream life of being "like" or "equal" to God. This was an offer she couldn't refuse. Then she got her husband to eat, as well.

THERE IS SAFETY IN SECOND.

What is rebellion? It is our desire to be "like" God or "equal" in authority. You see, Eve didn't want to be second place. She was actually very happy in second place, but the serpent tricked her into thinking that second place wasn't good enough. She couldn't settle for being second. All sin entered humanity at that point.

This is the sin nature we were born with. We want to be first. Look at every child ever. They really fight for first, then hopefully, they have parents that help them understand that their safety is in being second.

There is safety in second. Our culture says that if we're not first, we're last. When we buy into that, we start acting in rebellion to God's word. However, if we are willing to die to being our own god (rebellion) and simply tuck ourselves under the Lordship of Jesus Christ, we will rise victorious. We will be the kid sitting on Jesus' shoulders walking through the crowd with the best view, letting our dad fight our battles for us.

Many years ago, I was hesitating over a decision. I didn't want to do anything outside the will of God. The Lord told me, *"Jenny, if you are making a decision and really believe that I'm calling you a certain direction, I can fix those mistakes. You aren't going to make life-altering mistakes if you have prayed and genuinely believe you are being directed by me. If you rebel from me, that's where things are going to be pretty hard for you. That's where you leave the road of your destiny, and the consequences, although repairable, will get messy."*

That helped me to move forward and make decisions. If I felt it was God calling me, through prayer and confirming with the word of God, then I knew that I couldn't blow it if I was following him with an honest heart.

Rebellion will always cost us. When it comes to rebelling against God, we will know what that is because it involves going against what the word instructs us to do and not to do. When we read a scripture and say, *"Oh, that's so old fashioned. Things are different today. That doesn't apply to me,"* what we are doing is rebelling against God and being OUR OWN GOD. We are wanting to be "like" God or "equal" to God by establishing our own rules of good and evil.

This got Adam and Eve kicked out of the garden and Lucifer (Satan) kicked out of heaven. Anytime we want to be our own god, we suffer the outcomes of what our godliness can produce, which is nothing.

At any moment, you can turn to the Holy Spirit and repent. Repentance, as you know, is turning away from the road you were on — being your own god — and getting on his road as second to him. If we cannot do this, we will suffer the consequences and those consequences could cost us eternity. I'm not the judge of that, but I owe it to you to tell you that rebellion is nothing to play around with. It is also witchcraft (1 Samual 15:23) which has really bad fruit: sickness, poverty, emotional sickness, broken relationships, hardship, etc.

I want to point out something cool: when you study the second-born children in the Bible, you will see that many of them were favored. Just something to throw out there in case you ever want to look into that. Seconds are special. When we are willing to be second to God, we win and receive his blessing!

Lord, I turn from my own ways. I am ready to be second. Help me bow to you, knowing that you are the supreme Lord of my life. I tuck myself behind and into your loving leadership. Forgive me for going my own way and doing my own thing. Forgive me for ignoring your instruction in your word. I am ready to live a life of favor and blessing by following you. In Jesus' name, amen!

OUR SIN SHOULD HAVE KILLED US AND BANNED US FROM HEAVEN, BUT JESUS PAID THE PRICE ON OUR BEHALF.

8

THE MOST IMPORTANT PART

Since you have read this far, I am assuming that you want to experience God's best plan for you. You're at least very curious about it!

This is a dangerous prayer, but I believe that if you ask God to give you new life within, he will take you on a journey where you can let go of all that is already dead within you. Consequently, new life will spring forth within your calling!

However, we cannot move on until we have established the most important step to new life: handing your life over to Christ and inviting him to be your Lord and Savior.

Every single one of us was born into sin. Adam, the first

man ever created, handed down the sin nature to us through his disobedience. This is why our old identity cooperates with sin. We didn't start out as saints and then choose to become sinners. We were each born into sin from the beginning of our lives.

> When Adam sinned, the entire world was affected. Sin entered human experience, and death was the result. And so death followed this sin, casting its shadow over all humanity, because all have sinned.
>
> Romans 5:12 TPT

We have the choice to continue to live in our old sin nature or to empty ourselves of this old, wretched, selfish, stinky man and open up a new space for Christ to live within us!

The reason we have this incredible opportunity to die to the old and awaken to the new is because of what Jesus Christ did for all of mankind 2000 years ago. He was born of a virgin girl who was miraculously impregnated by the Holy Spirit. Jesus didn't have the DNA of an earthly father. His father was God.

You must understand that sin has a price tag: death. It's a spiritual law. Where there is sin, death must follow. There is no way to "do enough good things" to outweigh our sin and there are no "big sins" and "little sins." Even the most innocent-looking sin estranges us from God and requires death as a consequence. This death isn't limited to physical death and eternal hell. It includes death of relationships, death of the soul, death of our emotions, death of our sense of purpose, etc. Where there is sin that has not been submitted to Christ, there will be death in some way, shape, or form to follow.

Here's the Good News: God wasn't willing to let eternal death and separation from him be our fate! He created us for himself. We are his and he desires that all would come to a knowledge of the truth and be saved! He doesn't want anyone being separated from him and going to hell. Sin could have separated us from God forever but because of his pure love and affection for us, he made a way of escape!

> For sin's meager wages is death, but God's lavish gift is life eternal, found in your union with our Lord Jesus, the Anointed One.
>
> Romans 6:23 TPT

You might wonder why Jesus was qualified to be the special one to do the job for all of us. Well, he was the only man who overcame every temptation of sin. He was pressured heavily, just like you and me, but he stayed in fellowship with his Father, constantly praying and being in oneness with him. Jesus is our spotless lamb!

In the Bible, God put a temporary system in place to forgive sins (sometimes called the "Old Covenant"). The priests would take lambs, goats, and pigeons that were spotless (no flaws at all) and sacrifice them. It was a merciful covenant, but an animal was never going to secure eternal life. Only God himself would be the perfect sacrifice to take care of sin once and for all.

Jesus, the Son of God, knew that he came to die for every one of us. Our sin should have killed us and banned us from heaven, but Jesus paid the price on our behalf. He took all judgment of sin on his own body. Because he never sinned, he didn't have the wages of death on himself. Instead, he was able to lay himself down on that cross and say, "I'm going for them."

HE TOOK ALL JUDGMENT OF SIN ON HIS OWN BODY.

This huge death toll was unable to hold him hostage! He was resurrected to life after three days. His grave was found empty. No dead body! After this glorious resurrection, he walked the earth for forty days, visiting and sharing with his disciples. People saw him, talked with him and witnessed the holes in his hands from the nails the soldiers drove through his flesh. Then, he ascended into heaven and sat at the right hand of God.

The Bible says whoever calls upon his name and believes that their sins have been forgiven will be raised up to life as their old identity is buried.

> Everyone who calls on the Lord's name will experience new life.
>
> Romans 10:13 TPT

If you have never laid your life down to Jesus and put your faith in him, now is the time. Tell him in your own words that you don't want to carry your sins any longer, that you receive his full forgiveness, and that you want him to be the King of your life rather than yourself. Now is the best time to take this gift into your heart. Pause and pray, taking these words to heart and speaking them aloud. Use the QR code to pray with me.

Father God, I believe that you sent your son, Jesus, to die on the cross for all of my sins. I believe that he was resurrected on the third day, defeating Satan for me. I repent for all of my rebellion against you and I turn from being first in my life. I am committing to follow you, Lord. Thank you for resurrecting me to full life. I let you come into my whole being to be my Lord and Savior. I break every tie to the kingdom of darkness and receive every blessing that you have stored up for me. Thank you for new and true life. In Jesus' name, amen.

Congratulations and welcome to your brand new life! Look at what is now available to you:

> Our faith in Jesus transfers God's righteousness to us

and he now declares us flawless in his eyes. This means we can now enjoy true and lasting peace with God, all because of what our Lord Jesus, the Anointed One, has done for us. Our faith guarantees us permanent access into this marvelous kindness that has given us a perfect relationship with God. What incredible joy bursts forth within us as we keep on celebrating our hope of experiencing God's glory!

But that's not all! Even in times of trouble we have a joyful confidence, knowing that our pressures will develop in us patient endurance. And patient endurance will refine our character, and proven character leads us back to hope. And this hope is not a disappointing fantasy, because we can now experience the endless love of God cascading into our hearts through the Holy Spirit who lives in us!

For when the time was right, the Anointed One came and died to demonstrate his love for sinners who were entirely helpless, weak, and powerless to save themselves.

Romans 5:1-6 TPT

If you just prayed for the first time to give your life to Christ or made a renewed commitment, congratulations! This is your new beginning!

PART 2

EXPERIENCING TRUE LIFE

PLACES TO DIE

DIGNITY IS OVERRATED.

9

DYING TO DIGNITY

I grew up as a dancer. Dance was what eased the pain of my childhood. It had the miraculous ability to soften the blows of my parent's divorce and open my heart to new "moms and dads." It was incredibly healing for me.

I buried myself in dance and was able to lose myself there. Whether it was dancing down the grocery aisles next to my mom as she shopped or spending hours at the dance studio after school, I became dance. I was dance and dance was me.

When I entered junior high, my friends were all joining gymnastics, softball, or cheer. I decided that I didn't want to miss out on being with my friends so I quit dance rather abruptly. Cheer was the closest physical activity to dance that my school had to offer.

Several years went by and the love of dance faded off as a fond memory of my childhood. As a full-grown adult, the only dance happening for me was jumping up and down in a worship service or being a goofball in the kitchen to make my kids laugh.

SCARED TO DEATH

People may think I've never struggled with courage. This is simply not true. I've had to take on fear and insecurity just like everyone else.

One of the reasons I was a mess with Callie that day at the spa was because we had just booked our first women's conference and I could feel the date creeping closer and closer. Although I had imagined wonderful ministry and freedom taking place with the women in attendance, I had one vision that *scared me to death*:

"I want you to dance for me," I heard The Lord speak very clearly.

A terrifying scene of me dancing on the stage flashed through my mind.

"Ohhhhh no. No, no, no. That is a terrible idea. I can't be hearing you right. I am forty-three years old."

He wasn't letting up. *"Why are you scared?"*

This was beyond disturbing. I had gone through enough dying to disobedience to know that this was actually going to happen.

THE RESISTANCE

Here's Bernie, weighing in at a completely lifeless 130 pounds! A proverbial bell rang in my spirit. The wrestling match within had officially begun.

My newly revived spirit was overjoyed at the very thought of it. Dance is my love language!

But all too soon, Bernie stepped in with some of his counsel: "You're too old. You're too shy. People will lose respect for you. You're rusty, Jenny. You're not good at this anymore. And let's be honest. You're going to embarrass yourself."

I've mentioned this multiple times throughout this book, but we can't forget that the Bible says that our flesh and the Spirit are constantly at enmity with each other:

> For everything the flesh desires goes against the Spirit, and everything the Spirit desires goes against the flesh. There is a constant battle raging between them that prevents you from doing the good you want to do.
>
> Galatians 5:16-17 The Voice

My flesh was 100 percent uncomfortable with Holy Spirit's invitation to dance. At the very same time, I felt complete life on it!

Then I heard something that pierced my heart that I will never forget: *"I have a destiny for you Jenny, but it will cost you your dignity."*

DIGNITY IS OVERRATED

Taking one hesitant step towards this, I asked my oldest daughter, Hannah, if she would dance with me. She was in dance at the time and I thought this would be an easy yes. She didn't even take a breath before saying, "No." Feeling pretty pouty at that point, I said, "Thanks a lot."

That made me angry. I hit a pause right there. One tiny step in the right direction and I was already frustrated.

Then, one month before go-time, I attended a conference in New York City. The conference was incredible, but just like Galatians 5:17 says, I was at war within. I couldn't find peace. I was tossing left and right inside about this dumb dance. My spirit and my flesh were in an old western showdown.

That is, until Pastor Jentezen Franklin took the stage. In the middle of his message, he pulled up a scripture and beamed with a loud voice across the auditorium: "Let them **praise** his name with **dancing** and make music to him with timbrel and harp!" (Psalm 139:3 NIV, emphasis added).

Oh no. God is after me.

I felt it. Of the thousands of people in the auditorium that day, I felt as if Pastor Franklin was only talking to me.

The Holy Spirit was beaming within me: *"Jenny, will you PRAISE his name with DANCING?"*

I heard this question reverberate inside of me: *"DANCING? DANCING? DANCING? DANCING?"*

He then began unpacking the lyrics of a newly-released worship song at the time, "So Will I." His message and impartation of the lyrics cut me open:

> If the stars were made to worship, so will I
> If the mountains bow in reverence, so will I
> If the oceans roar your greatness, so will I
> For if everything exists to lift you high, so will I
> If you left the grave behind you, so will I
> If you gladly chose surrender, so will I

This moment marked my life. It was as if heaven opened up for me and the scales were tipped in the favor of the Spirit within me. My flesh shrank back in pathetic defeat.

I could almost feel the cold, lifeless body of Bernie hit the boxing ring floor with a loud and weighty bounce. Holy Spirit within me stood beaming from ear to ear, gloves raised in the air.

Hillsong Worship, "So Will I," (Songwriters: Joel Houston, Michael Fatkin, Benjamin Hastings) January 5, 2018, CCMG, 12 on *There Is More*, 2018

Victory filled the atmosphere of my inner man! My spirit declared, *"If everything exists to lift you high, so will I!"*

I danced for Jesus at our first Her Voice Conference in Portland, Oregon. I let go of what people thought of me and praised him that day, worshipping in full abandon. I just didn't care about anything other than my spirit being free to lift him high.

The Cambridge dictionary defines the word "dignity" as calm, serious, and controlled behavior that makes people respect you.

Ironically, when we give up our "controlled behavior" or desire to be seen as dignified in the eyes of others, he gives us a new dignity in return. This dignity is not based on the accolades or praises of man, but on the affirmations and security that can only come from God.

THE MULTIPLIED SEED

As we've learned, if we are willing to die in one area, we can expect to see a multiplication of life as a result. This is exactly what happened after I danced.

You see, my daughter, Hannah, had been in a long, stubborn season of resisting the invitations and prophetic words she had over her life as a worship leader. She told me, "I'll never do that. I'll never sing in front of people. No one can make me."

As her mom, I was perplexed as to why she was so scared. She had an incredible voice and I didn't understand where this deep-seeded resistance was coming from.

The day that I danced, I had this flashing thought: *I bet that when I take this step of dying, that resistance will break off of her.* It was as if Holy Spirit was saying, *"Watch how this works. You go first and watch the freedom be multiplied."*

> **THE DAY I DANCED, I WASN'T THE ONLY ONE WHO BROKE FREE.**

That's exactly what happened. It wasn't more than a few weeks later that her flesh lost a several-year-battle with fear. Her spirit rose up and she hasn't stopped singing privately and publicly since.

    I know without a shadow of a doubt that my resistance had been empowering her resistance and now, my freedom was empowering her freedom. The day I danced, I wasn't the only one who broke free.

    Just like a seed, we multiply! One appleseed never produces just one apple! When we allow ourselves to break out of our seed packets of safety and go down into the deep, dark, and scary soil of obedience, we will burst forth with fruit upon fruit …. and more fruit! Who knows how many other men and women have been inspired by Hannah's freedom and have found their own freedom in return?

    If we have to forfeit our dignity before men in order to obey God, so be it! Others will watch our freedom and catch it for themselves. Our dying is never just about us!

PRIDE MUST DIE IN YOU, OR NOTHING OF HEAVEN CAN LIVE IN YOU.

10

DYING TO PRIDE IN MARRIAGE

> "Pride must die in you, or nothing of heaven
> can live in you."
> Andrew Murray, *Humility: The Journey Toward Holiness*

A sweet couple sat next to Bob and me at a dinner function. They had been married for just three days. They looked very innocent and had probably enjoyed the best three days of their life. Both of them had an extra sparkle in their eyes.

After a pleasant conversation about their wedding and getting to know them a bit, the wife leaned in a little closer and asked my husband and me, "What is the number one piece of marriage advice that you could give us?" She asked this with excitement and anticipation of something they could hang onto for the rest of their lives.

"Die."

With zero hesitation, it just came out of my mouth. I didn't even look up from my plate.

Silence.

I could tell it didn't quite land. They were perplexed. I attempted to explain.

"The only way this works is if you die to yourself and live for the other person. That's all. That's the best advice I have. You can struggle and demand that your spouse give you what you want and somewhere along the way, you'll realize it's not about what you want out of the marriage. It's about serving the other person's needs."

I went back to eating. They sat, still confused.

I decided to leave it at that.

There was no way to truly explain to these two love birds how this whole thing would shake out in a few short weeks.

> **THE ONLY WAY THIS WORKS IS IF YOU DIE TO YOURSELF AND LIVE FOR THE OTHER PERSON.**

PRIDE REVEALED

We don't really know how selfish we are until we get married.

If we have pride in us, it will reveal its ugliness sooner or later. Nothing has taught me more about my own pride and its impending death than being married. If you can win the war against pride inside your marriage, I believe pride will have a much more difficult time thriving outside your marriage.

REJECTION

We bring the way we perceive ourselves into our marriage. For me, I came into our marriage with a lot of wounds. I was extremely sensitive to feeling rejected and overlooked. This was because I hadn't healed from my parent's divorce and this wounding had followed me into my marriage. Of course, I didn't know that.

Because the rejection wound was so deep, I saw everything through the lens of rejection. When Bob wanted to go out with friends, I was rejected. When Bob didn't want to sit and talk for hours, I was rejected. I had heard that most men typically don't want to talk for long periods of time, but I had a stronger belief that Bob was rejecting me than the belief that men didn't have the same amount of words as a female in one day.

I went to marriage seminars and took notes on all the marriage tools, nodded my head, and went home to try and do them with everything in me! But, because I didn't see myself as loved, the tools from marriage conferences only went so far. I was still suffering from abandonment and I didn't know my identity in Christ. Eventually, the rejection would override all that I had learned and I would go back to my old ways of demanding love and attention. (My husband is going to have a big reward in heaven for sticking this one out.)

STRIFE

One night, I was sound asleep when I heard the word "strife." I woke up and couldn't fall back to sleep. It was loud in my spirit! God had my attention. I got up and walked into my office because my spirit was bothered. I didn't have the peace I needed to fall back asleep.

Sitting in silence, I could feel that the Lord was wanting to discipline me. I knew I was being called out for the strife I was responsible for in our home. Like a child that realizes what he or she has done, I came to the humbling realization that I was causing our home to be at war. I was acting in strife, which is rebellion to God.

Unity is where God commands the blessing:

> How truly wonderful and delightful it is to see brothers and sisters living together in sweet unity!
> It's as precious as the sacred scented oil
> flowing from the head of the high priest Aaron,
> dripping down upon his beard and running all the way down to the hem of his priestly robes.
> This harmony can be compared to the dew
> dripping from Mount Hermon,
> which flows down upon the hills of Zion.
> Indeed, that is where Yahweh has decreed his blessings will be found, the promise of life forevermore!
>
> Psalm 133 TPT

I CAME TO THE HUMBLING REALIZATION THAT I WAS CAUSING OUR HOME TO BE AT WAR.

A significant piece of this scripture that we should take note of is the picture of the unity flowing from the head priest (the head of the household) down to the other members of the household. This is a picture of how attitudes (good or bad) flow from the top of any family or organization to the rest of the members. This is where we become extremely accountable in marriage.

I told God that I wanted to be put on a short leash. God doesn't literally put us on a leash, of course, but my desire was to give him permission to stop me before I went on making a bigger mess of things. Are you familiar with retracable dog leashes? I could just imagine myself running wildly around a tree, then a car, then God-knows-where-else. I didn't want to make a big mess and then go, "Shoot, how do I get untangled from this mess I've made?"

That "short leash" request was a good one. It started a new way of living for me. I would feel the Holy Spirit's gentle tug, hearing him say: *"Don't say that." "Delete that text." "Go say you're sorry."* These corrections were immediate. I wouldn't get one smidge into my flesh and the Holy Spirit would bring correction.

HAVING THE LAST WORD

After this "strife" wake-up call, I began to repent. This is when God instructed me to bite my tongue and he made it very clear: *"Die to having the last word."* Oh man. That was a big one for me. *"But what if Bob says something unkind or untrue? You want me to just let that fly?"*

You see, in my flesh, I felt like Bob was getting away with something if I didn't bring truth or correction. But I felt God really press in on me to let it go. He impressed on me that he (God) would get the last word if I would be quiet and give him room.

I can honestly say Bob and I have rarely fought after this. Once I didn't have to rebuttal everything and appease my flesh with saying what made me feel right and good, we didn't really have anymore explosive arguments. We've had heated discussions, but nothing where it got out of hand and brought division.

I had no idea that having to have the last word was causing so many problems for us. But if you think about it, having to be right and having to have the last word is totally about pride.

Now, if you are facing an abusive marriage, you need to get help immediately! I am not referring to this degree of dysfunction. But as for a marriage where two people are trying to figure out how to live in unity and harmony, these are truths to grab ahold of.

I struggled with the fear that I would just disappear if I wasn't heard and understood. Again, this is about rejection and abandonment. I wasn't sure if I could trust God to defend me or advocate for me. I didn't have any context for a person sticking up for me. I didn't have the trust or understanding with God that he would defend me and help communicate to Bob in a way that I couldn't. This really came down to being humble enough to trust God.

> **THIS REALLY CAME DOWN TO BEING HUMBLE ENOUGH TO TRUST GOD.**

If you're married, what has your marriage revealed about you? Have you seen any childhood wounds attempt to pervert the relationship you have with your spouse?

THE REMEDY

I came to realize that the more I spent time journaling with God, conversing with him and allowing him to love on me, the more I was able to relax and not try to defend myself at every turn. As I let go of the fears of being alone, abandoned, and rejected, our marriage became a fun and trusting friendship.

Because pride is rooted in fear, and fear creates distance between us and God, spending intentional time with him is very purifying. Fear has a tough time sticking around when we feel loved and safe in God's presence. He loves you, and if you know that deeply within you, you will be able to walk away from pride as your self-protection.

Let's practice. The Holy Spirit wants to build you up. Let's see what happens when you just sit in the presence of God and simply allow him to love on you — that's right — just like you would sit with a friend at coffee or lean on a friend's shoulder for a hug.

Put a timer on for five minutes and get as relaxed as possible. Start out by just telling him you want to be with him and seek his voice for love and encouragement. Tell him you want to know what is on his heart for you. Tell him you want his guidance and friendship. Tell him you want correction.

One question you might ask him is, *God, what do you want me to know right now?* Listen and wait for a thought to come to mind. Be patient and relaxed. Ask God if there is more that he would like you to know. Use this QR code for more guidance.

After sitting in God's presence, what did you sense, feel, or experience? Was it hard, easy, awkward? Tell the truth.

_____

_____

_____

_____

_____

_____

_____

_____

_____

_____

LOOK AT GOD. HE WAS THE ONLY PERFECT PARENT AND ADAM GOT IN A BIT OF TROUBLE.

11

DYING TO PRIDE IN PARENTING

"Here is the path to the higher life: down, lower down! Just as water always seeks and fills the lowest place, so the moment God finds men abased and empty, his glory and power flow in to exalt and to bless."
Andrew Murray, *Humility: The Journey Toward Holiness*

MOTHERHOOD IS NOT FOR WIMPS

"Mommy, what's wrong?"

I was a ball of tears in the middle of the afternoon, laying in my bed with my covers completely over my head. Frustration and failure had caught up with me and I felt miserable about myself and the interactions I was having with my kids.

"Nothing," I mumbled.

"Mommy, I can hear you crying." Esther wasn't convinced. She peeled the covers slowly back so she could see my face. "What's wrong?"

"Mommy doesn't feel like a very good mom right now." I'm pretty sure my bottom lip was quivering.

"Mom! You are the best mom in the world!" She laid her head on my chest and wrapped her arms around me.

This wasn't the first time I felt like a big fat failure as a mom. In fact, this was an area that I had felt extremely discouraged and disappointed in for an extended season. My insecurities, which were rooted in pride, were being triggered left and right through teenage and toddler tantrums. I felt completely out of control and defeated.

Because I had bought the lie that I was failing at motherhood, I would hear through that filter of failure. Bob would say, "Are you making dinner?" I would hear, "Are you neglecting your motherhood responsibilities again?" Bob was simply asking the question so that he could plan to make something. My pride, manifested through insecurity, perverted an innocent question to an accusation.

> **REALIZING THAT MY MOTHERHOOD LENS WAS SMEARED WITH DECEPTION, I KNEW I NEEDED THE TRUTH TO SET ME FREE!**

Realizing that my motherhood lens was smeared with deception, I knew I needed the truth to set me free! I asked the Lord about this and he said, *"Every time you even have the slightest thought that you are failing or you hear an accusation, say, 'I'm a really good mom.'"*

For the next two weeks, I would say this randomly when I felt defeated. I warned Bob that I was going to be saying this whenever the lie was coming at me. What is quite incredible is that I had to say this statement consistently for about two weeks. After two weeks, I actually believed it. *I am a really good mom.* I never went back to believing I was terrible at it. This two year battle with motherhood insecurity was settled in less than two weeks by declaring the truth.

Second to marriage, motherhood has been the most profound place in my life that has caused me to confront my pride. In my case, pride was masked in insecurity, failure, and disappointment. Being a parent lends itself countless opportunities to be confronted in our pride. Here are just a few areas where I discovered that dying is the best option. My advice to you, mothers, is to do the same: die.

Die to a full night's rest.

Die to the lie you have believed most of your adult life that it takes eight hours of uninterrupted sleep to have a good day. If you don't, you will be perpetually frustrated. I can't tell you how many times I have awakened in the morning and said, *"God, you are my energy. You resource me with all the energy I need for the day."* I love a good night's sleep just like anyone else does! But when that doesn't happen, we can still have a fantastic day if we will breathe in God and let go of fear… fear of being tired. Literally imagine yourself letting that go. Why use energy wrestling with that? Remember my painful contractions that manifested through fear?

If we are trapped in a negative mindset from lack of sleep, we may need to humble ourselves (die to the pride of not getting our way) and ask God to help us. Leaning on God for help takes humility. Pride says, *I should be able to hold myself up.* Humility says, *I cannot hold myself up. God, will you hold me up?*

Die to the idea that you should be able to keep a perfectly clean house.

Die to the lie that a perfectly clean house means that you are succeeding as a parent. Success isn't defined by how clean our house is. Success is defined by how obedient we are to the Holy Spirit (because we're getting this dead thing down, woohoo!). A clean house is wonderful, but it shouldn't have the authority to declare you as a loser or a winner in the arena of life.

I've let a messy house ruin too many of my moods and that's just a problem with my thinking. There's something about a mountain of laundry that just humbles me. I have to tell myself, "*It's okay. God is good. Breathe, Jenny, breathe.*" (Can you tell which area of my life God is still using to help me die?)

If your family is like my family where messes are made faster than they can be cleaned up, get help. Pay for help. This will be invaluable for you. I am not able to function for very long in disorganization, so I pay for my house to be cleaned every so often and I also disciple my kids to clean up after themselves (which is not quite as effective as paying someone, let's be honest).

Die to "your" schedule.

WE HAVE TWO AVAILABLE RESPONSES AT OUR DISPOSAL WHEN "OUR" SCHEDULE GETS WIPED CLEAN: WE CAN REMAIN COMPLETELY FLEXIBLE AND GRATEFUL TO SERVE OUR FAMILY, OR, WE CAN THROW A FIT.

Just when you are sitting down to work on a project, your fifth grader tells you they have a project due tomorrow and they need eighteen items from the store. Not only do you go to the store at 10:00 p.m., but you actually *do* the project for him because he needs to be in bed. Many of us have been here, haven't we? Or, how about the midnight interruptions, text messages asking you to come pick them up without any advanced notice, or that vacation you had planned until your little one got sick?

We have two available responses at our disposal when "our"

schedule gets wiped clean: we can remain completely flexible and grateful to serve our family, or, we can throw a fit. A fit could be verbal and aggressive, it could look like stonewalling, or, it could be passive aggressive. It's anyway you behave so that others will pay the price for "what they've done to you."

What I want to highlight here is that you may notice this being a place in your life that you prefer to cling to. Maybe you are rigid with your time? Some people have a very difficult time letting people into their schedule. Some people schedule themselves so tightly that they haven't planned for any error or margin in their day. This creates frustration because life keeps interrupting what they have perceived to be "their schedule."

Many years ago when I had gone through a big "house cleaning of the soul," I asked God if there was anything else that I needed to give him. I couldn't think of one more thing that he would want me to give up. After all, I had purged so much rebellion and intentional sin from my life! I waited for a split second and he said, *"Yes. I'd like you to give me your schedule."*

Now, to tell you that this intimidated me is an understatement! Giving up partying, cussing, and all that junk was easy in comparison to this request! My schedule? What would he possibly ask me to do with my day if I wasn't in control of it?

This was a tough one for me. Then, I started having children and that began the beautiful process of letting go of my own life. But you know what? The more I let God interrupt the nap I thought I "had to have" and all the little particulars of my rigid schedule, the more joy and freedom I experienced. He has blessed me with opportunities, relationships, and inner joy that I wouldn't have if I had remained tight as a top. It all goes back to letting go, right?

Die to your weaknesses.

If you are the mom that reads all the school emails or pulls the notes out of the backpack and combs through every word, you are my hero. Even after five kids, I could never get that down. I'd kill it the first week of school and then somehow, start sucking at it for the rest of the school year.

I wanted to label myself as a terrible mom for not keeping up with the kid's schoolwork, but then I became older and wiser and discovered that I needed to die to being amazing at everything. I just let myself off the hook and decided I could be average in this area. I'll do my best and forget the rest. Humbling, and it feels great.

I think I'm pretty good in areas that matter to me like teaching my kids spirituality and making sure they know they are loved by God and by me. I'm pretty good at encouraging them to go after their dreams. I'm not *perfect* at it. I have nights where I want the family to read the Bible together and it's like World War III breaks out. The dog poops on the rug and a little person hits another little person.

Part of this is spiritual warfare, (we'll deal more with spiritual warfare later), but the point I'm making is that we have to die to the idea that "this moment was supposed to be perfect." When you get to the end of this chapter, you will see what our aim is. Hint: it's *not* being great at everything.

Whether it's schoolwork or Bible reading, we need to come to terms with the fact that we are going to have weaknesses as a parent. Need someone to help your child through math and you can't pull it off? Hire help. Do whatever you need to do to help your child, but don't get caught thinking you are supposed to be as good as the parent you see on social media. I promise you, that momma has her flaws, too. We all need help somewhere and that's a good thing!

Die to guilt for not being a perfect parent.

I was riding on my exercise bike one day and sobbing to the

Lord that I must have really messed up as a parent because my teenage daughter was really struggling at the time. She was battling insecurity and fears that had me twisted up in knots on the inside. I was lamenting before God, *"What did I do wrong? I should've done so many things differently."* I was feeling like such a failure! I carried so much regret.

The Holy Spirit quieted me. I could sense he was about to respond.

When I heard what he said next it brought me relief and correction at the same time, the way that only he can do:

"Jenny... get over yourself."

Something lifted.

"She's my daughter. This is between her and me. This has nothing to do with you."

Whoa. Suddenly I could see how I was spiraling into selfishness and making her life journey about me. Then, I saw a vision. I was standing at the gravesite where a body that *looked* like me, but *wasn't* me, was laying in the grave. "Perfect Mom" was in the casket being lowered into the ground. Holy Spirit and I had a ceremony and buried this unrealistic mother that wanted a place in my life.

The Lord said, *"She's not real. She never was. Die to that false image."*

> **"JENNY... GET OVER YOURSELF."**

Something heavy snapped off of me! I suddenly became free of the guilt of failing my daughter somehow. I swallowed my pride and realized that she was walking out what we all have to go through: a struggle with who we are and Whose we are. This was between her and God. I would pray for her but I would never make her life choices about me and my failures again. I can't tell you how free I became that day!

God allowed me to play out the "what if" scenario…

"Jenny, what if you were a perfect mom, never making any mistakes, helping your child be happy twenty-four seven, never being short or making a single mistake in their eyes?"

That sounds dumb now that I think this through. But the worst part is that, if I were to fulfill her every longing, she would never have any reason to reach out to God in need. Desperation is what brings every single one of us to God. We hit that low place and realize that nothing and no one else can fulfill us except for God.

Some of us have this belief, that if we could only be perfect parents, our child would not be experiencing hardship or sin. Look at God. He was the only perfect parent and Adam got in a bit of trouble.

Die to the desire to impress other people with your family's outward appearances.

Bob drives separate from me to church. We have two services so he heads out much earlier than I do. I do my best to get all the kids peeled up out of their beds, dressed, and out the door. Some days my two youngest girls, who can't get themselves fully ready yet, look incredible. They have adorable clothes and because they are still young, they love to match their outfits.

Other days, it looks like I picked them up off the side of the freeway. I don't know where their shoes go while we're all sleeping. I have no idea where their hairbrush is and sometimes I just pray my way through the house looking for stuff. They insist on wearing the pink leggings and I find myself digging through the laundry wondering if I'll be late, *again*.

What I *do* know is, whether or not they look cute to the world, they are so adorable to me. I believe in good hygiene and dressing well, but I don't go too far on this one. If we're putting more effort into how they look in public than what we are putting into their hearts, we need to readjust.

This is one of the things I've enjoyed about being an older mom (I had my last two over 40 years old). I just don't care as much as I used to about how my family looks in the eyes of other people.

With age, some of this dying gets easier.

Die to the dreams *you have* for your children.

I had a dream that my kids would all want to love God fiercely. I still do. But when they become teenagers, they have their own free will to make their own decisions about Christ apart from Bob and me. We have to die to controlling their journey. God told me to get on my face in prayer because this was about the only thing that I could do to influence them towards a relationship with him (apart from loving them well and modeling my own radical love for him).

My oldest daughter began the journey of finding her true identity and her love for Jesus in her late teens. She told me that, when I stopped meddling with her relationship with Christ, she was able to desire him for herself.

> **WE HAVE TO DIE TO CONTROLLING THEIR JOURNEY.**

If you want your kids to play a sport they don't want to play, why? If you want your kids to love something that you love but they are showing no interest, it's time to let that go. If your kids aren't the best on the team but they are having fun, can that be okay with you?

We have to be careful not to live out *our* dreams through their lives. God has dreams for you! He has dreams for them! The best thing we can do for our kids in the area of their dreams is to ask them what is in their heart to do in life and then go after our own dreams. There is power in modeling.

As my kids have become older teens, I have really enjoyed helping them navigate what they believe they are called to do by God. I went to college, but none of my teens have shown interest in that. They want to build businesses and go to ministry school. (Wait, that sounds like us. Again, modeling is influence.) Life is too short to worry about what our kids will do with their lives. Start asking questions about what interests they have and then start problem solving with them to find out how you can help them make that dream come true.

My oldest daughter has a fashion line centered around her art called "Heaven Designed." As a little girl she would draw on everything including her brother and the furniture. She was a little hesitant to start this business, but I spent time encouraging her and got her around other people in the same industry to inspire and mentor her. On my part, it has been time and energy well spent.

LOVE IS OUR MANDATE

Everything grows out of one of two trees (root systems): love or fear.

Pride is rooted in the tree of fear. Dying to fear is *very* important for parenting (and marriage). If we parent out of a place of fear and pride, we will not lead well. We will not experience the true joy of parenting because we'll be riddled with worry and anxiety. Fear is torment and separates us from love, especially the love of God.

Love is the principle thing that our families need from us. If we want to operate in pure love, we have to make room for it by dying to all this stuff that truly holds no value.

Love is one of the many gifts that we get in exchange for dying. If you carefully read 1 Corinthians 13, you will see that Paul describes love this way:

Love
(1) is patient under stress,
(2) is kind at all times,

(3) is generous, not envious,
(4) is humble, not self-promoting,
(5) is never rude,
(6) does not manipulate by using shame,
(7) is not irritable or easily offended,
(8) celebrates honesty,
(9) does not focus on what is flawed, and
(10) is loyal to the end.

When I read that list, I am inspired to become more like Christ for my family. I am not where I want to be yet, but I know I will become more and more loving the more I am willing to let go of pride.

Read that list one more time and just imagine this being a description of your marriage and your family! Dying has remarkable rewards.

> So above all else, let love be the beautiful prize for which you run.
> 1 Corinthians 13:13 TPT

YOU ARE ONLY HURTING YOURSELF WHEN YOU RESIST YOUR CALLING.

12

DYING TO CALLING, CAREER, AND FINANCES

One of the hardest places to die to our own will is in the area of our life's work, or, our calling. This is usually connected to how we spend our time, our talents, and how we earn our income.

Within months of me praying the "dangerous prayer," we received an invitation to be on a call from our company's headquarters. On the call, they informed Bob and me that the primary way we were being financially compensated was going to be removed from the company pay structure.

We had built our business over twenty years and had become one of the top five income earners in the company. We were well established in the industry. This is what we had known and invested our lives in. We lived in our dream home, drove the cars we wanted to drive, had five kids involved in multiple activities, a church to care for, an itinerate ministry, and a partridge in a pear tree. Now, just like that, 99 percent of our income was going away. We had to figure out what in the world we were going to do next. To say we were shocked would be an understatement!

We had the opportunity to become bitter, resentful, and afraid. That would have been extremely easy. But we knew that God was still in control and offense and bitterness would only ruin us.

> **WE KNEW THAT GOD WAS STILL IN CONTROL AND OFFENSE AND BITTERNESS WOULD ONLY RUIN US.**

Oddly, I felt relieved. I didn't understand that at all, especially as I looked at my dream home and realized that this was all going away very quickly.

Leading up to this, I had dreams of being caught in an avalanche, a burning cabin, and other extremely disturbing scenarios. I had a feeling these dreams had to do with our company collapsing, but I dismissed these thoughts. A business of twenty years collapsing didn't make any sense. (This was before I trusted my discernment as much as I do now.) Looking back at these dreams, I can see that the Lord was preparing me for what was coming.

WHAT IS GOD DOING?

Now what? The only thing Bob and I heard the Holy Spirit say was, *"Be still and sell everything."*

The very *last* thing you want to do when you know your income is going bye-bye is to *be still*. You want to do just about anything but *be still*. You want to find a source of revenue quick-like. God wasn't rushing that part.

Friends reached out to us with gracious invitations to look at other avenues and opportunities. We didn't get the green light on any of it. They would've been lucrative. They would've saved us from having to sell our home and cars. We prayed and waited to get a green light, but it just wasn't happening! They were great opportunities but we could feel the Holy Spirit putting us on pause. Red lights. That's all we got when our phone was ringing with opportunities. We desperately wanted God to just fix it. Then we wouldn't have to lose anything. But we could feel it. This wasn't what the Lord was doing.

We knew that he was shifting us into a new life space. I could feel the peace come over me as the Lord was asking us to leave the life we were familiar with and join him on a new adventure.

THE FIRST GREEN LIGHT

We put our house up for sale and waited for an offer. Meanwhile, my friend from Alabama, Ann, sent me a text with a real estate listing. The listing was for a retreat center sitting on fifty acres in Corbett, Oregon, just thirty-five minutes from our home in Portland! I opened the listing and read about the history. The more I read, the more I became curious.

We asked our realtor to schedule a tour. Now, let's just stop here and consider how ridiculous this was. We didn't have the funds to buy this property in full. We would need a loan. Who in the world would loan two people a large sum of money when there was no income coming in? This seemed so ridiculous that I had a suspicion God was in it. The main feeling I had was God prompting us to be curious enough to explore the unknown.

THIS SEEMED SO RIDICULOUS THAT I HAD A SUSPICION GOD WAS IN IT.

Stepping out of my car onto the property for the first time, I felt myself submerged in prayer. I could feel the decades of prayers that had been prayed on this property.

It had been a kids camp since the 1950s and needed a ton of

updating. Bob was walking around with his eyebrows furrowed together. I knew he was looking at windows that needed replaced and structures that needed reinforced, not to mention all of the cosmetic updates. Still, I felt the Holy Spirit's approval on this. I had no idea how this would happen, but I was open to how God would sort it out.

REWIND A YEAR PRIOR

The crazy thing is, I had a dream about this place one year prior.

In my dream, I walked into the basement of the main building and it opened up to an arena that I knew was an equipping university. It had been neglected and was up for sale. I looked up in the ceiling rafters and hundreds of canoes were toppled over one another with spider webs, rust, dust, and decay all over them. I knew that the canoes were for the students sitting in the bleachers. (The arena was actually inverted so that the center stage was lifted up and the bleachers cascaded down from the stage. The students would sit with their backs to the stage and their eyes fixed on the content that was being cast to the outside walls by the handful of professors who were teaching from the platform.)

In the dream, I knew that if we purchased the equipping center, Bob and I would have to reach up in the rafters and grab the canoes one at a time, scrub them clean, polish them, and send out pairs of students into the world. I could feel the gravity of the work and commitment it was going to take. Still, I turned to Bob and said, "We need to buy this place and get it up and operating." He asked me if I knew how much work we would be getting ourselves into. Honestly, I knew I didn't. I couldn't wrap my mind around how much work it would be. I just had a strong sense of anticipation.

The dream ended with Bob saying, "Here's another option. We

can grab one canoe, scrub and clean it up, and row ourselves out of this dream." That still makes me laugh.

MAKING A MOVE

So here we were, standing in the reality of a dream I'd had a year before our business collapse. I couldn't see how the income would come through and I couldn't put the pieces together in a way that made sense, but I could feel the Holy Spirit breathing on it.

We decided to make an offer and ask the owners if they would carry the loan for us.

"No."

That was our answer. Okay then, moving right along.

I didn't think twice. I washed my hands of it and decided to keep moving. Then, our realtor said, "You need to write them a letter." A friend texted me the same day and said, "You need to write them a letter." I randomly read a testimony Shawn Bolz had shared about writing a letter for their building and how God had moved miraculously on their behalf.

Three confirmations. Okay, fine. I'll write a letter. Can I just say right here that I'm not one to write letters and beg people for stuff. Again, Jenny would need to die to her pride right here. So, I sent them a letter.

THE LETTER

The letter was our story of doing ministry for years, losing our business, and desiring to equip the saints for the work of the ministry on the property. We explained our history of ministry so they understood that we had been in ministry for years, but the main gist of the letter was that we wanted them to pray and ask God again if this was his will. We told them we wanted to carry on the legacy of prayer and ministry that they had started decades ago.

Crickets.

Meanwhile, we were showing our house and getting offers, but the closings were falling through. We were like, *"God, are you there? What on earth are you doing?"* We didn't feel we had any other option than to just believe.

Then, one day in prayer, I was expressing a little frustration to God about not hearing a response back from the owners of the retreat center.

I said, *"Lord, they really should do this for us. We told them that we would carry on the legacy of the gospel in this place. I know we will make every payment. Why aren't they responding?"*

"If you were them, would you do it?" The Lord swapped roles and wanted to know if I would carry a loan if I was in their shoes.

"Absolutely."

This was not hard for me to answer. I knew we were good for it and that lives would be radically changed there. This was a no-brainer. I would do this for them if it were me!

YOU CAN'T MAKE THIS STUFF UP

"Jen, we got an offer on the house." Bob called to tell me the news while I was on a layover. "There is only one thing.... They wrote a really great letter. They are asking us to carry the loan for them. And they are asking if they can purchase it with everything in it."

"Wait. Everything? What do you mean by everything?"

They meant *everything*: pictures; decor; chairs; tables; bar stools; coffee tables; end tables; beds; mattresses; dishes, and sheets.... yes, sheets. Really nice sheets. I was floored. I had Restoration Hardware couches and dining room table. It was tough for me to imagine ever having those things again.

I read the letter and couldn't believe it. A woman named "Jenni" and her husband, along with their five kids, were asking for this home. They stated in the letter that they could tell that we loved the Lord and wanted to continue this legacy in our home.

Wait, *my* name is Jenny. *I* have five kids. *I* wrote a letter asking for a loan. *My* letter said that I wanted to continue the legacy of the Lord.

God had asked me if I would say *yes* to a letter requesting a loan. When I answered *yes* to his question in prayer, I believe it triggered a kingdom transaction. We said *yes* to Jenni, and within days, the owner of the retreat center wrote to say they would carry our loan. We hadn't heard from them for *months* and suddenly we were under contract.

DYING TO A SMALLER VISION

We began packing... *very little*... and Bob got to work on the lawn.

When we first moved into this house, I had asked Bob if he would plant grass where the kids could play. As it was, the backyard was mainly just dirt. Bob disagreed and said he didn't want to maintain a lawn. I decided not to fight that one out and let it go.

Now, I was standing outside watching my husband work diligently on a lawn for "Jenni." He was very proud of how it was coming in so green. I watched him water and tend to the lawn for days. I didn't say anything but it really started getting to me. *Wrong Jenni, Bob. This is the Jenny you were supposed to plant grass for.*

One mid-morning, I realized that this grass thing was really eating at me. I stepped outside to the edge of the newly planted yard and stared across it. I was grateful that Jenni would have grass, but the effort Bob was putting into a lawn for her was really unnerving me. So, I did what I do every so often: I asked the Holy Spirit into a staff meeting with the wise side of me and the flesh side of me.

As I stared out at the lawn, I felt the Holy Spirit standing there with me. I asked him, *"Why does this bother me so much?"*

I didn't hear a response. Instead, an image popped up in my mind: two gigantic lawns, as large as football fields. These were the lawns at our retreat center; the retreat center that God had found favor with us to influence the owner to say yes to us purchasing.

"My bad."

How had I forgotten that I was moving to a fifty-acre retreat center where my kids would have acres to play on? I was only looking at what I was losing and had completely forgotten what I was gaining. I had gotten caught up in feeling ripped off for a minute. I turned around and walked into the house as all feeling of loss and agitation dropped off of me.

We've been ministering to people here at Crestview Conference Center for two years now. We have seen hundreds of people get saved, delivered, healed, set free, and equipped. The university of equipping is truly underway. The youth here are also thriving. There is a movement among the "Gen Zs" that cannot be described in words. Also, I didn't think we would do kids camps… I was pretty wrong about that. We've had a move of God since the day we arrived and it hasn't stopped.

WE WERE STRIPPED DOWN AND PRUNED DOWN SO THAT WE COULD BEAR MORE FRUIT.

God has not allowed us to miss a single payment to the owners. We've been introduced to the most incredibly generous people in this mountain town. They are people ready to serve, help our team "clean canoes," and love us well.

Meanwhile, God has brought my husband and me not only one business, but two more businesses. We were stripped down and pruned down so that we could bear more fruit (John 15).

I've become convinced that we should not follow our own plans when it comes to our calling.

I love the Apostle Paul's story. He had made it his life's work to torment and kill Christians until he found himself on the road to Damascus where suddenly, a bright light blinded him and he was knocked to the ground. He heard the words, *"Saul, Saul, why are you persecuting me? It is useless for you to fight against my will"* (Acts 26:14 NLT). Another translation says, *"Saul, Saul, why are you persecuting me? You are only hurting yourself when you resist your calling"* (Acts 26:14 TPT). God changed Saul's name to Paul and Paul was transformed from being a passionate Christian killer to a passionate Christ lover! In fact, Paul wrote a huge portion of the New Testament!

There might be a time in your life when God calls you to the next thing. What you have to believe, by faith, is that if he calls you to it, he'll bring you through it. And you know what? He is GOOD! I wouldn't trade this new life for my old one. That was a great season and I've moved on to a greater one.

Has God called you to move on to another season? Do you find yourself clinging to your calling or career, making it your identity? If so, this may be another place of trust; of dying; of allowing God to bless you and take you higher. If you are resisting the CALL of God to move into greater territory, then we may need to hear what God told Paul, *"You are only hurting yourself when you resist your calling."*

God knows what is best for you. He knows what will fulfill you and cause you to depend on him more. Can you trust him with your calling and your finances?

Take a moment to pray. Ask the Holy Spirit if he has your calling secure, your finances in his care, and your career in his plans. He will answer you.

Just *be still.*

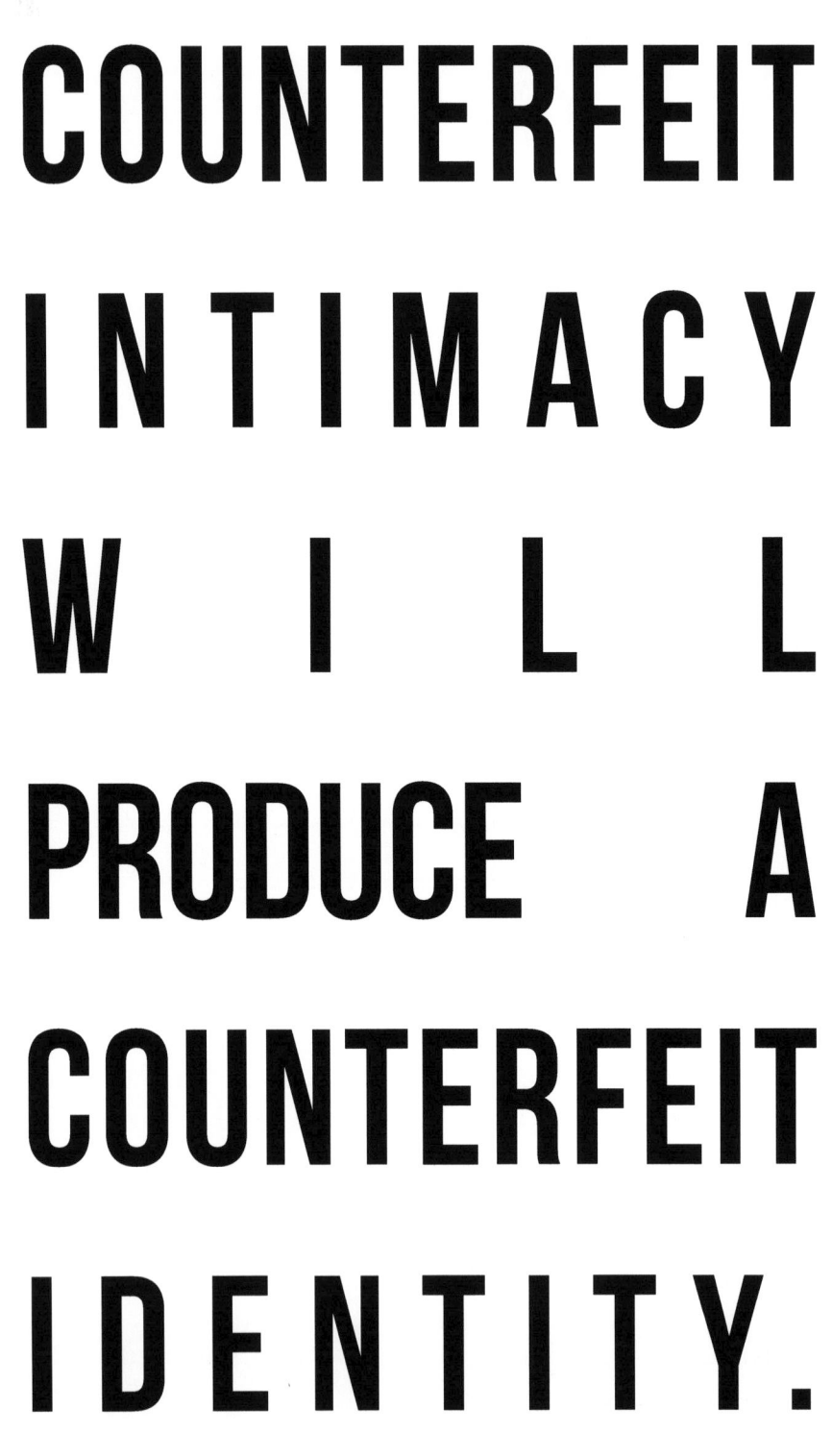

13

DYING TO COUNTERFEIT COMFORT

We all have a deep need for comfort. The Positive Words Online Dictionary defines comfort as:

To be in a comfortable state where one feels at ease or relaxed.
Something that makes us feel relaxed or at ease. Example: a comfort blanket or a comfort toy.
Pain relief or somebody, something that relieves anxiety.
To cheer somebody up. To put someone in a state where they feel at ease or relaxed.

It's really not surprising why humans sin. Most of the time, we're looking for comfort. Seeking comfort is absolutely not a sin!

It is a necessity. How we choose to find comfort is where sin might show up.

YOU DON'T HAVE A "COMFORT ZONE"

Whether we are experiencing deep loneliness or bravely following God into new kingdom territory, we are usually simultaneously trying to preserve our personal comforts. Our comforts can be physical, emotional, financial, or relational. Comfort can come in all sorts of ways! Most of us have said, "That is out of my comfort zone," or "I have to get out of my comfort zone."

One day, when I was heading out into uncharted territory, the Lord said to me, *"Jenny, you don't have a comfort zone. If I am 'Comforter' and I am with you wherever you go, how can you be out of your comfort zone? I AM your zone. I AM your comfort."*

I got excited. I could feel courage and relief come over me. He continued speaking. *"What you do have is called a 'familiar zone.' You are unfamiliar with many places and things we will do together. Even though you may be unfamiliar with where you are and what you're doing, make no mistake about it, you are not out of your comfort zone because I AM your Comforter."*

Wherever we go, we are in our comfort zone because the Comforter himself goes with us wherever we go!

THE PROBLEM

This seems so simple, right? Just lean on the Comforter and you're good to go. But there is a problem we have to tackle first: we actually have to let go of our counterfeit comforts to embrace the Comforter himself! There is an exchange that has to take place and it's up to us to decide if we will let go of our *false comforts* and cling to the Father.

For example, maybe you really like making people happy and that has gone too far into making sure that people are pleased with you at all times in all circumstances. What are you going to do when God asks you to stand in political conversations and use your voice in a way that opposes what others are voicing? You would have to sever your commitment to people-pleasing because this new territory won't offer that comfort. You would have to shift your commitment over to pleasing God rather than man.

So, how do we truly shift from the counterfeit addictions of popularity, selfishness, drama, gossip, monetary status, material wealth, drugs, social media, pornography, getting our way, being first, and vanity, (just to name a few)? Although the answer is simple, it is not necessarily easy because our comforts have become our pacifiers. Taking a pacifier away from a baby isn't complicated. It's simple. But it's not easy!

Here's the simple answer: shift your gaze and go "all in."

DETACH AND ABANDON

Detach from worldly comforts as your source of so-called "strength" and abandon yourself to the person of Jesus. He is not a religion or a belief system. He is a person. He is with you now. He is the Comforter. He is waiting for you to call on him and rely on him for everything.

This is simple and yet, very challenging. We are used to using counterfeit comforts to pacify our struggles. We've uncovered this truth in scripture a few times already, but it's worth absorbing over and over again. Look at the blessing we receive from God as we detach from the world and abandon ourselves to God:

> The person who loves his life and pampers himself will miss true life! But the one who detaches his life from

this world and abandons himself to me, will find **true life and enjoy it forever.**

John 12:25 TPT (emphasis added)

True life! That's what we get! Not a false, counterfeit life. And that's not all... *we will enjoy it forever.*

How do we abandon ourselves to God? It starts with a decision that is made at the heart level. This cannot be an intellectual decision we make in our own strength. Just like you cannot commit yourself to marriage only with your mind or intellect. It's a heart level commitment to surrender your whole self to God.

Here is a place to start: put your whole self (mind, body, and spirit) onto God. Morning, noon, and night, make him your focus and deepest commitment. Decide and declare, *I am going to go all in with Jesus. I am going to detach from the lies that have never truly comforted me and let him come to me and fulfill me. I am going to give him a fair chance to be my everything. If I have Jesus, I have everything I need.*

START THE SHIFT

Now shift. That's it. Shift from throwing yourself into a bunch of things that cannot ultimately satisfy or give you comfort, counsel and correction and throw your gaze upon him.

You can start by reading the Bible and letting the scriptures wash over you. Meditate on the words you read! Read them aloud. Pull out a highlighter and mark the words in your Bible that jump out to you. Ponder those words. Ask the Holy Spirit questions about what you are noticing. Read the footnotes.

Put on worship music and fix your heart on him. Out loud, tell him how much you need him and want him. Sing a song of joy while you wash the dishes. Turn off the radio during a drive and begin to tell him about your day and ask for his advice and wisdom.

Go on a Jesus date with a notebook and ask him to give you wisdom to grow your business before you come up with your own plan.

You can do this. I believe in you. God believes in you.

One warning, however: you're not doing this so that you can be seen as a religious or spiritual person. You have a spirit, so you are already spiritual. The reason you are doing this is so that you can experience the true life that Jesus spent his life to give you. When you are in this type of oneness with God, you will experience true life.

This is why the Bible is very clear about us not clinging to our lives, even unto death (see Revelation 12:11). If we aren't willing to lose our lives (our soulish comforts), then we won't even get in the fight. We won't contend for our promised land. We'll just sit on the sidelines and spend our time protecting our stuff.

HIDDENNESS

The key to experiencing true life with true comfort is hiding ourselves in God.

There are many Bible verses that lead us to a place of hiddenness with God as our place of strength. Some refer to this as our "secret place." This is a sacred place within us where we can intentionally enter into communion with God and only God. Our spirit unites in oneness with his Spirit and the entire world goes quiet as our awareness of him captures our attention. We shut off the valves that open to the outside world and intentionally open our hearts inwardly to a hidden sanctuary with God.

Without this sacred secret place, I would not be the person I am today. It has radically changed who I am and has made me who I am.

> When you abide under the shadow of Shaddai,

you are **hidden** in the strength of God Most High.
He's the hope that holds me and the stronghold
to shelter me, the only God for me, and my great
confidence.
Psalm 91:1-2 TPT (emphasis added)

Never underestimate what can be accomplished in and through us when we become determined to be hidden in God.

Susanna Wesley knew how to hide herself in God against all odds. She had nineteen children and her husband would leave for days at a time. This made it almost impossible for her to find the time and space to pray in her secret place. That didn't stop her. She would throw her apron over her head at odd times throughout the day. When her apron was over her head, her children knew that she was praying and couldn't be disturbed.

Two of her sons, John and Charles, grew up to be powerhouses for God! At the age of seventy, John Wesley preached to nearly a million people and delivered the gospel message of salvation to 32,000 people without the use of a microphone! His brother, Charles, wrote over 9,000 hymns, many of which we still sing today.

It's been said that William J. Seymour, who started the Azusa Street Revival in 1906, would stick his head in a stack of boxes as he kneeled to pray. I'm sure this looked weird and foolish to people watching, but if you understand what happens between God and the person in the place of hiddenness, you totally understand why he walked in so much power. His ministry led to revival meetings that lasted through 1915. Thousands of people experienced miracles and came to know Christ, and many churches are active today because of his relentless devotion to hidden prayer.

William was seeking God's heart and shutting out the world in order to hear what God wanted to say and do. He was shutting out the world and shutting in the Holy Spirit by putting his head in those boxes! He knew that he couldn't do anything in his own strength or skill set, but only by the power of the Holy Spirit. Connecting deeply with the Holy Spirit requires a decision to be hidden in him.

COUNTERFEIT INTIMACY

I have learned that we *all* lock our gaze on something or someone. In other words, we all enter into hiddenness with something or someone. When we hide ourselves in anything other than our Jesus, we are setting ourselves up for defeat.

Remember when the Israelites escaped Egypt? They came to a dead end at the Red Sea with no way to cross as Pharaoh's army was closing in behind them when God split the sea in half so they could walk across! Thousands upon thousands of Israelites made it safely to the other side. As for Pharaoh's army, well, things didn't go so well. As soon as the Israelites were safely on the other side, the waters swallowed them up. Every single person in Pharaoh's army drowned and just like that, 400 years of slavery came to an end. Can you imagine?

Just two weeks after this miracle, the Israelites began to get restless. Perhaps they didn't know how to be free because they had never been free before. Their forefathers had passed down their instructions: inhabit the Promised Land that God would give them. They were supposed to walk right on through the wilderness into Canaan where there was lush property and food in endless supply. This was supposed to be a ten-day trip! The wilderness was dry and lonely and had no decadent comforts whatsoever.

Instead, they doubted. Even after they saw the Red Sea split; even after they saw a cloud appear to supernaturally guide them through the wilderness; after they saw fire appear before them at night; and even after they saw food appear on the ground every single morning, they didn't know how to worship this invisible God who did visible things. They decided to make for themselves a golden calf that they could worship tangibly.

Forty years went by (they got a bit distracted) and now they had finally arrived at the border of Canaan. They sent twelve spies to go in and see the land for forty days and nights. All twelve men came back reporting how the Promised Land was absolutely over-the-top incredible. But ten of the twelve men *also* gave the report that they would not be able to apprehend the land because the giants were so big that they were but mere "grasshoppers" in their eyes. They were overcome with intimidation and decided that they were already defeated and led hundreds of thousands of Israelites into a ceremony of defeat. They all wailed and cried because these ten men gave them the report that *WE CAN'T DO IT.*

There were two other spies, Joshua and Caleb, who completely disagreed with the other ten:

> But Caleb tried to quiet the people as they stood before Moses. "Let's go at once to take the land," he said. "We can certainly conquer it!" But the other men who had explored the land with him disagreed. "We can't go up against them! They are stronger than we are!"
>
> Numbers 13:30-31 NLT

Sadly, the Israelites believed the report of the ten spies and celebrated defeat before they even attempted to enter the Promised Land. All of the adults who agreed with the negative report spent their entire lives unto death in the wilderness. They never entered into what God called "a place of rest," their promise of abundance.

Joshua, Caleb, and all the minors *were* allowed to cross over! Why did Joshua and Caleb have a completely different response to the giants than the other ten spies? They stood in the middle of hundreds of thousands of people wailing in defeat and interrupted the majority to say, "No, we can surely do it!" Can you imagine doing this?

If we want to be able to say *WE CAN DO IT* in the face of our giants blocking our Promised Land, we must know where Joshua and Caleb got their courage from.

If we back up and trace the lives of Joshua and Caleb, we can see that they were worshipping God in the wilderness, not a shiny cow (or any other dead object for that matter)! They had heard the same thing that everyone else had been told for centuries - that God had promised to give them land. They just stuck with the plan that God had laid out and didn't veer from it with the rest of the crowd.

The Israelites had become intimate (hidden) in a dead, shiny calf. That's really sad because their promise was literally right under their noses and God told them he'd give it to them! In the face of those giants, the shiny calf offered them no strength.

We will all become intimate with something. What we become intimate with, we identify with, and that will be where we draw our strength from in time of need. There will be a day when you and I are going to find ourselves standing at the border of our own personal Promised Land. We are going to have an opportunity to take the land and believe that God will kill every giant in our path. Ultimately, we will either see ourselves "like grasshoppers" and claim defeat before we even try, or, like Caleb, we'll say, "We can do it!" The one we choose will all depend on *who* or *what* we've hidden ourselves in during our wilderness seasons.

During the dry, dark, and painful seasons of life, it is easy to grab something that brings a temporary high to be intimate with: shopping, vanity, material wealth, popularity, sex, alcohol, and the list goes on. What we behold in our hearts (what we hide ourselves in) will become what we believe we look like. Our identity will be defined by what we behold. The question is, will what we are beholding lend us the strength we need in the day we need it most?

Counterfeit intimacy will produce a counterfeit identity.

The spirit of intimidation that is on the loose in our country is at an all-time high. We don't feel that we have options for freedoms that are rightfully ours, so we bow. Why? Why do we bow to intimidation? *It is because we see ourselves as grasshoppers!* Why do we see ourselves as grasshoppers? Because we haven't hidden ourselves in God and instead, have hidden ourselves in something dead and lifeless. To feel strong, we have to worship someone who can provide strength. We will only get as much strength as the *who* and *what* we worship.

SWARMING LOCUSTS

In the first few months of the COVID-19 pandemic, I had a dream where I was swatting huge locusts that were swarming through the air. I was dodging them because I didn't want them to touch or harm me. They were big and obnoxious.

The Lord led me to the passage of scripture in the book of Revelation where locusts came swarming out of the smoke and were given authority to sting and torment people for five months. There was a group of people who didn't get stung.

> And out of the **smoke** appeared **locusts** swarming onto the earth, and they were given authority like that of scorpions to inflict pain. They were told not to harm the grass, or any green growth or any tree, but only to afflict those who did not have the **seal of God on their foreheads.** The locusts were given authority to torment them for five months, but not to kill them. Their painful torment is like the scorpion's sting, and during that time people will seek death but will not find it; they will long to die but death will elude them.
>
> Revelation 9:3-6 TPT (emphasis added)

When I read this passage, I had to dig for more. Here is what I discovered in the TPT footnotes:

> a. 9:3 Locusts emerged from the **smoke**. The smoke of the abyss is a picture of deception. The lies of the enemy are a "smoke screen." The **locusts** are a picture of the words, actions, and lies of the religious system that dominates and intimidates others (Nah. 3:17). It causes others to feel inferior, like "**grasshoppers**" (or "locusts"). See Num. 13:33; Joel 2:1–10; Matt. 3:4.
>
> b. 9:4 The **forehead** is a metaphor for our thoughts, our minds. We must have the seal of **sonship** on our thoughts, the seal of God as our Father, or we will be tormented in our minds over our true identity in Christ.

Notice in the footnotes, the swarming locusts came from deception and come to torment and sting with intimidation. If there is anything swarming through the air of our land in our day, it is a spirit of intimidation! From governmental intimidation to cultural and religious intimidation, people are getting stung by this evil spirit. When we are intimidated, we bow to a false authority. This is what the Israelites did. They bowed to the giants, a false authority.

Here is what jumped off the page at me: the people who were protected from the sting of intimidation were those who had the seal of sonship. What is sonship? It is the identity that we hold firmly inside of us that we are sons and daughters to Father God. We are not slaves to a harsh taskmaster. We are not bowing to a religious system because God is our Father. He is everything a father is supposed to be: a provider, comforter, counselor and a protector, to name a few.

If I see myself as a slave rather than a son (or daughter), then I will bow to another authority. But if I see God as my authority, I won't bow to a counterfeit giant because I'm under the authority of my Father.

This is where Joshua and Caleb were set apart. They had been worshipping and beholding God as their Father for years so they weren't deceived by the "smoke" of lies that the giants were too big. Remember how the other ten spies described themselves as little puny grasshoppers in the eyes of the giants? Sounds like they got stung.

Caleb was described as one who had a "different spirit" because Caleb knew who he belonged to. He knew he was a son. The sting of intimidation flew right past him. Do you want to be like him? Let's pray together for the seal of sonship:

Lord, I want to know you as Father. I don't want to know you as a religion or distant ruler. If I am under your care as my Father, I won't be able to bow down to a fake. Give me a different spirit like Caleb! I want to go wherever you lead me, even where it doesn't make sense and the scenery is unfamiliar. You are not just 'the Comforter,' you are MY Comforter! There is none other who can satisfy my deep need for comfort like you can. Lead me into rest wherever we go. In Jesus' name, amen.

OUR GIFTS HAVE A DARK SIDE.

14

DYING TO STRENGTHS AND GIFTINGS

Sitting in my chair for prayer one morning, I felt the Lord leaning in to give me some instruction.

"Jenny, I'm going to start a new journey with you. I will begin by lifting up the rug and one at a time, things that are not of me are going to be exposed. Some of them are in your kids, some are in your church, some are in your marriage, and some are in you. If you will square up to each one as I expose it, I will eradicate it immediately. If you turn even slightly another direction to avoid the confrontation of it, it will grow and multiply."

I was getting a "big girl talk" from my Father. I imagined furry little monsters crouching in intimidation, looking up at me as the Lord lifted the corner of the rug. I sensed that his timing was at hand. It was time to square up to every problem that "had always been there" but was not in my present awareness.

And so it began. One at a time, these icky things began to crawl out of hiding. Instead of buckling in disappointment or panic, or explaining them away in positivity, I dealt with each problem head on and heart forward. (After all, he distinctly said that if I didn't square up when they were exposed, I would see one monster become many. This was very motivating to stay on the "big girl" course!)

> **INSTEAD OF BUCKLING IN DISAPPOINTMENT OR PANIC, OR EXPLAINING THEM AWAY IN POSITIVITY, I DEALT WITH EACH PROBLEM HEAD ON AND HEART FORWARD.**

POSITIVITY TIME OUT

As issues were brought to my awareness, I was tempted to make excuses for them for the sake of "being positive." My husband and I had built our family and church culture around faith and positivity. No gossip aloud. No slander. No complaining. No questions asked.

One of the monsters in particular was a situation with a friend who was complaining about me to our mutual friends when I wasn't around. A few of those friends came to me and said, "We can't take it anymore. She's constantly complaining about you when you're not around. Even if she doesn't use your name, we know she's talking about you."

My heart sank. My first reaction was pain, but I quickly moved on in attempt to make myself feel better about it. Time to get positive people! I reasoned to myself, *I'm not entitled to be talked about nicely all the time. It's okay. People have a right to their own opinions. I'm not going to say anything because maybe she needs to vent.*

God confronted me in this.

"Jenny, just because I gave you the gift of positivity doesn't mean

that it is helpful to use anytime you want. In this case, you are using it as a shield to protect yourself from pain. I would like you to submit your positivity and all of your gifts and abilities to me so that they can be used appropriately. This is not an appropriate way to use positivity. Let's confront this issue head on."

I realized in that moment that I had been using my gift of positivity to avoid what really needed to happen: loving confrontation.

I called my friend and said that we needed to meet and talk through what had been brought to my attention by our mutual friends. The conversation wasn't easy, but it was simple. God told me to come at every ugly issue squarely, firmly, and in love so that it could be dealt with and resolved. She admitted to all of it and apologized. I left the meeting feeling like I was living in truth rather than smoke. Deception from the friendship had been removed.

I'd love to tell you that this friendship was healed and we were able to grow closer together because of the honesty that was put on the table that day. Sometimes this is the outcome of these mature confrontations.

That wasn't the case this time. Our friendship struggled after that and eventually ended.

I had sensed for a long time that God didn't approve of this friendship for me, but I couldn't imagine my life without her in it. We had so many great times together! Still, I sensed something unhealthy that I couldn't put my finger on. I had been ignoring a gift that was very appropriate to use in this scenario: my gift of discernment.

In the big scheme of things, this relationship was toxic because the gossip was divisive in our church body. This was an attack on unity. The Bible says that a house divided will not stand (see Mark 3:25). My friend didn't realize that she was being used as a pawn of the enemy to splinter the trust in our culture.

Just so we're all clear, this is a demonic spirit! This is not about a person. The Bible is clear that we don't war against flesh and blood, but against a powerful class of demon-gods and evil spirits in the atmosphere (See Ephesians 6:12). We will address spiritual warfare extensively in future chapters!

HOW ABOUT YOU?

What are your gifts? What are you known for? What comes easily to you? So easily that you don't even have to think about it?

Is it possible that you are using your gifts in ways that work best for you rather than submitting them to Christ for his purposes?

> **IS IT POSSIBLE THAT YOU ARE USING YOUR GIFTS IN WAYS THAT WORK BEST FOR YOU RATHER THAN SUBMITTING THEM TO CHRIST FOR HIS PURPOSES?**

It hadn't really occurred to me up until this point that my gifts weren't there to use anytime or anyplace that I wanted. God was saying, *"Put away your positivity for this situation. Submit it to me so that I can remove something that is toxic and poisonous to your life."*

If you look at this situation from a 14,000 foot view, you will see how God is good. In my pea-sized understanding of my life, I thought this friendship was a good thing. In hindsight, I see that God wanted to cleanse my life of things that were toxic!

When it comes to your gifts, would you be willing to die to the idea that these gifts are yours to use whenever and however you want?

MAXIMIZER MADNESS

I want to give you one more example of why we need to die to the ownership of our gifts and submit them to the leadership of the

Holy Spirit.

In the *CliftonStrengths Assessment by Gallup*, thirty-four innate strengths (or talents) are identified. When a person takes the assessment, they receive their top five strengths. They are the ones so wired into the person that they may not even realize they are there. Gallup says that these talents don't change with time, circumstances, or beliefs. They are wired in and that's that.

One of my top five strengths is maximizer. A person with the gift of maximizer will spend their time looking for ways to transform something strong into something superb. Maximizers love perfection and love to polish something that is already shiny. It's all about taking something from great to greater! Can you see how this gift could be very dangerous if it's not submitted to God?

I remember a time when I was ten years old and my mom asked me to clean my room. I emerged six hours later excited to reveal to my mother how I had labeled my clothing rod with little signs that said "white shirts," "pink shirts," and so on. Everything was in unrealistic and unattainable order. My mom looked alarmed and decided not to ask me to clean my room much after that.

This obsession with perfection would drive me mad! I remember painting an acrylic cat for my art project when I was fifteen years old. It was due the next day and I ended up painting the entire night because the nose wasn't quite right, then the ears were off just a little, then I didn't like the color of the eyes. FIX. PAINT. FIX. REPAINT. ALL. NIGHT. LONG. (Insert crying emoji.)

It was five o'clock in the morning. I had a half-inch thick cat that looked like he'd been run over ten times. Not only had I just pulled an all-nighter, but I was sobbing at the look of this sadly abused cat. It was awful.

The truth is, my maximizer gift had taken the lead and run me and the cat right off a cliff. At this age, I had no idea how to pull the reigns on this gift and say, *Maximizer, give it a rest.* Actually, I had no idea that this was a gift. I was just trying to make a perfect cat, after all.

GIFTS GONE BAD

Our gifts have a dark side. When we don't submit them to the leadership of the Holy Spirit, they tend to go on autopilot and lead our decision making. They are not to be used like a kid playing in the knife drawer, grabbing aimlessly in curiosity to see what can be stabbed and cut. Knives used in wisdom and submission are helpful, but without applying wisdom, they can be dangerous. Knowing your gifts and strengths is so important so that you don't get taken for a crazy ride when they jump ahead.

With this maximizer strength, I have to constantly be aware of its dark side. I will catch myself not making even little, small steps of progress if I can't finish it to perfect completion.

For example, I will look at a messy kitchen and think, *How long will it take me to sweep, mop, scrub, windex, dust, reorganize the shelves and clean out the fridge?* I've had to learn to tell my maximizer gift to *sit this one out* so I can just put some dishes in the sink, wipe down some counters and move on.

I have been grateful for this gift, but it has also caused me pain when I haven't submitted it. I often have to ask the Holy Spirit, *"Is this something you want me to maximize?"* Then I wait for him to say *yes* or *no*. It has become that simple.

LAY 'EM DOWN

Maybe it's not the gift of positivity or maximizer that you have to lay down. It could be the strength of a warrior you have within you that wants to rise up and fight every battle. Maybe it's the gift of silence and solitude that you will have to surrender. God may require you, like he did Queen Esther, to risk death to speak up on behalf of a family or a nation. I don't think that's too far fetched as I observe where our country is at this time in history. Are you willing to lay down your gift when the Holy Spirit says there is a greater one to pick up in its place?

I had to learn how to handle the passion and fire within me. I can be easily triggered to draw my sword at the smallest hint of trouble. I have a lot of fire in me and my flesh tries to take some of it for itself at times. I like being fired up, but I've had to learn to submit it to the use of the Holy Spirit. This fire inside is now preserved just for God!

I HAVE A LOT OF FIRE IN ME AND MY FLESH TRIES TO TAKE SOME OF IT FOR ITSELF AT TIMES.

When we don't die to our gifts (submit them to God and use them as he directs), we become subject to them. When we *do* die to the ownership of our gifts, we experience exceptional fruit! People are blessed by them! You are blessed by them! When a gift is laid at the feet of Jesus, he gets to decide when you get to use it and when to set it aside for a time.

WAKE UP, SLEEPY GIFT

Another one of my strengths, according to the *CliftonStrength Assessment*, is communication. This means that I can easily put my thoughts into words and that it is easy for me to present and communicate. This is the strength you are experiencing right now because you're reading this book. But it wasn't always like this.

You see, up until a few years ago, I had danced around the prompting of God to write books. I would argue with him that I didn't think anyone would want to read what I had to say. I would see books written about similar content and think that was a good excuse to not write about the same subject.

God was also asking me to get on Facebook Live. I was absolutely terrified to do this. I didn't know "how." After lots of excuses and procrastination, the Lord still hadn't forgotten about it.

He was still there asking me to do it.

I remember the first time I went live on Facebook. I had educated myself on the communication strength and decided to dust it off and give it a go. I was used to using this gift in live presentations but not talking into a camera. I had to die to my excuses and let the gift rise up and take me there. I just decided to push the LIVE button and start talking. Some of those early videos back in the day have more views than the videos I do now. When God is calling you to do something, he isn't going to leave you high and dry. If it's his idea, he has something in mind to make it all work. Sometimes, you just have to do things afraid and trust God more than your feelings.

YOUR TURN

You are so uniquely made, so powerful and equipped. But, do you *really* know what gifts you have and how to use them appropriately? When we are unaware of our gifts, we forfeit our effectiveness.

Take the time to learn more about your strengths by taking a gifting test that you've learned about. When you get the results, don't just read the results and move on. Dive into the components of the gift. Read up! Study them. Open up the hood of the car and see what these wonderful gifts are all about. If you are uneducated or unaware of your gifts, you won't be able to enjoy their maximum blessings and avoid their dark sides.

BE DILIGENT TO FIND OUT WHAT MAKES YOU SPECIAL.

If you don't know where to start, research the *CliftonStrengths Assessment* and be sure to read all of the reports that come with it.

Be diligent to find out what makes you special. Strengths are like the tools laid out on a surgical tray for a surgeon to use during a medical procedure. It would be detrimental for a surgeon to choose a tool at random, or worse, not know how to use the tool! Your gifts are your tools and the Holy Spirit is your guide. Seek and pray for wisdom!

In the same way that a surgeon has access to a variety of tools, you have access to a variety of gifts. For a positive outcome, a surgeon must use the correct tool at the correct time in the correct way for the correct reason. Just because a surgeon has access to a scalpel and knows how to use it doesn't mean he or she should use it on every procedure! Just because you have a gift and know how to use it doesn't mean that it is appropriate to use in any situation that comes to you.

What gifts do you have that come naturally to you?

_____

_____

Text the following message to two or three friends who you trust to tell you the truth (or feel free to rephrase the text in your own words):

> "Hi! I am in a book study called
> 'Wake Up Dead' and I have an assignment
> to ask an honest friend to answer this question:
> What would you say a few of my gifts are?
> From your observation, what do I do that
> helps the world around me to be a better place?
> Thank you so much for your feedback.
> I will learn a lot from this!"

What responses did you get?

How did they make you feel?

What did you learn about yourself from their feedback?

Have you taken any personality or strengths tests? What were the results?

How are these gifts a blessing to you and others? Give an example of how one of your gifts has produced Godly fruit in your life.

What is the dark side of these gifts? How can they backfire on you or others when used inappropriately?

Do you have a gift or strength that you have laid down, and

now the Holy Spirit is prompting you to pick it up again? How is he asking you to execute this gift?

_____

_____

_____

_____

Envision yourself submitting your strengths over to God. See yourself following the leading of the Holy Spirit when you feel him nudge you to lay down a strength or pick one up again! The fruit of submission is life and blessing to you and the people you influence. I encourage you to pray this prayer:

Holy Spirit, I submit all of my gifts to you. After all, they come from you and they ultimately belong to you for your purposes. Thank you for blessing me with these incredible gifts. I am so thankful to have them to bless the world and build the kingdom of God. Please bless me and my family with my gifts and let not one of them be used to damage or hurt me or others. Please help me become a master at my gifts by giving me education and knowledge about how these gifts work and are useful to you. Send me resources and people to teach me more about them. Please show me when each of my gifts are needed and when they need to be set down and set aside. Guide me to use the right gift at the right time for the right reason. In Jesus' mighty name, amen!

PART 3

WARFARE

LAY DOWN TO RISE UP

THE DEVIL ISN'T NICE AND HE DOESN'T PLAY FAIR.

15

WARRIOR, RISE UP

We are in a war. Many westernized Christians don't really understand this. Maybe because we don't *want* to be in a war, we feel that it makes us *exempt* from war? Or, perhaps we do know that we are in a war, but we don't really know how to engage in battle. As westerners, we tend to explain life, both good and bad, through natural cause and effect.

In many other countries, people are well-aware of how the spiritual world impacts our natural world. Talking about angelic and demonic activity is not a strange conversation to them!

In the United States, "spiritual warfare" is usually something reserved for a small handful of elderly ladies in the church who fight in the Spirit on behalf of the church.

While I absolutely believe in having a designated group of intercessors for our churches, I don't believe that the rest of us should pass on the responsibility to war in the Spirit just because someone else is doing it for us! This is a critical part of Christianity. You and I were enlisted into a war. Don't you want to know how to fight?!

> Be well balanced and always alert, because your enemy, the devil, roams around incessantly, like a roaring lion looking for its prey to devour.
>
> 1 Peter 5:8 TPT

IGNORANCE IS NOT BLISS

The devil hopes we will stay ignorant to this. He hopes you won't read this whole book. If you read it, he hopes that you don't actually die to your flesh and get trained up as a soldier. He wants you to be a weak, untrained, "nice" person who wears a Christian t-shirt to show your faith.

HE WANTS YOU TO BE A WEAK, UNTRAINED, "NICE" PERSON WHO WEARS A CHRISTIAN T-SHIRT TO SHOW YOUR FAITH.

Please hear what I'm saying! I love Christian t-shirts! I wear them and sell them! That said, while wearing a t-shirt with a Bible scripture on it is great, it's *greater* to have that biblical revelation deep inside of you that causes the enemy to flee in frustration.

If we think that Christianity is primarily about trendy fashion, good music, and meeting new friends to do life with, we're eventually going to get bombed spiritually. We become an easy target for the enemy when we are ignorant. We can't figure out why our marriage is scratchy, why our teenager is depressed, and why we keep getting sick. Ignorance is *not* bliss in this arena.

The devil isn't nice and he doesn't play fair. He doesn't look at your young child and think, *I should go easy on them since they're so young.* If anything, that's when he lays it on thick. He likes to attack us when we're in our most vulnerable state.

If people really knew the battle between the kingdom of darkness and the kingdom of light being waged *over their own lives*, they would urgently desire to learn how to access and use the weapons they have access to.

You may need to die to the paradigm that Christianity is about having a war-free life. No, my friend, when you became a Christian, you enlisted into the army of God. We need you trained up and ready to fight the good fight.

YOU WERE ENLISTED INTO AN ARMY

Imagine that you are at the recruiting office. They hand you a uniform and send you out the door to your assigned location.

When you arrive to your assigned location, war is breaking out. You notice that some of your fellow soldiers have incredible weapons and are skillfully using them to attack the enemy. You also notice that a bunch of you don't have any weapons at all. Sure, you can hunker down in the bunker so that you don't get hit, but you don't have a gun, hand grenades, or any other type of offensive weapon.

You are thankful to be with soldiers who have weapons, but you also wonder why they got them and why you didn't. You can't help but think how much safer and more victorious your regiment would be if every soldier had a weapon and knew how to use it.

While we were all enlisted into battle when we gave our lives to Christ, not all of us were equipped with weapons and training. While the Bible is clear that we are to disciple people once they receive Christ (see Matthew 28:19), not all of us have received discipleship in the area of spiritual warfare. I think the church is moving into a season of discipleship. We have to!

BEFORE WE BEGIN

You can frighten the enemy! Do you know this? Don't think for one minute that you should be scared of this fight. In fact, it is just the opposite. The enemy is freaking out and trembling that you are reading this and getting trained up as a mighty soldier!

YOU CAN FRIGHTEN THE ENEMY!

What you have to understand is that Satan was defeated when Jesus went to the grave! Jesus went to hell and suffered the punishment that you and I should have suffered. Because he was sinless, hell could not keep Jesus down. He overcame all defeat and rose back to life on the third day. He remained on the earth forty more days after his resurrection, interacting with his disciples and giving them more instruction (to disciple the nations!), then he ascended into heaven and sat down at the right hand of the Father.

Because Jesus took on hell for us, we are no longer subject to the punishment of hell or any assignment from hell by demonic activity. If we are suffering from the devil's torment in our lives, he is trespassing and you and I have been given the authority through the death and resurrection of Christ to call him out and cast him out (see 2 Corinthians 5:21; Acts 2:24; Matthew 28:18-20; Mark 16:15-18). I just want to jump and shout right there!

TERRITORY

When Satan has planted himself in an area of our lives, we experience turmoil. How do we take back this territory? How did he get ahold of it in the first place?

In his blog article, "How to Break Satan's Strongholds in Your Life," Adrian Rogers describes it this way:

> I know there are many Christians who have

a satanic stronghold in their life. It's harming them, wrecking their spiritual life, contaminating the life of their family and church. The devil has found an unclean place within and built a foul nest, a beachhead, a stronghold there. And he uses that stronghold to war against God and His work.

Ephesians 4 says, Neither give place to the devil… and grieve not the Holy Spirit of God. We should sit up and take notice: on the one hand we could give place to the devil, and on the other, grieve the Holy Spirit. Either one should be unthinkable What does it mean to "give place to the devil"? Let's say you own 50 acres of land and I ask to buy one acre right in the middle of it. You sell it to me, so now I have the right to go in and out of your property at will in order to get to my one acre.

Suppose I start throwing trash around and playing loud music all hours of the night. I'm desecrating your property, but there's nothing you can do! You've given me access. When you try to make me leave, I say, "I'm not going, and you can't make me go. I've got a legal right to it. If you don't like it, tough luck." You wouldn't be able to move me out because you gave me a place there.

Some of you have done the same thing for Satan! You can't dislodge him unless you dislodge him legally because you've given him a place. He owns some strongholds in your life.

In the following chapters, we are going to address how to dismantle the enemy legally, but for now, I want to spend a little more time revealing the gravity of spiritual warfare in your life and how it can hide and diminish us without us realizing it.

MY LAUNDRY ROOM

A few years ago, we fixed up an eighty-year-old home on our retreat property. The basement was dark and grungy with two bedrooms and no windows. We put in new carpet, tore up the old disgusting bathroom and gave the walls a fresh new coat of paint.

My two oldest teens were excited to establish their cave dwellings here with paints, crafts, game systems, and far-too-many thrifted clothes. It wasn't long before paint had spilled on the new carpet and random crafts and trash were spread all over. This basement would be considered a Martha Stewart nightmare.

The first year we lived in the house, I had this idea that we could have some type of neatly arranged laundry system. With seven people, it can get out of hand so quickly. Unfortunately, our washer and dryer were smack dab in the middle of this chaos.

I did everything: begged, pleaded, yelled, made chore charts, threatened, bribed, grounded, and punished. I would go downstairs and my blood would boil (insert cartoon image of steam blowing out of my ears). I could be having a wonderful day! Then, I'd walk into my laundry-room war zone and it would set me off like nothing else. On more than one occasion, my husband lovingly told me to go read *Still*, the book I wrote about finding rest in the middle of chaos a few years ago. This is sad, but true. With so much training in peace and rest, how had the enemy seized the authority to send me to another planet?

HE WAS REROUTING ME BACK TO WORSHIPING HIM AS THE SOURCE OF MY PEACE.

I let this go on for far too long before finally asking God what on earth we could do to get this laundry area under control.

"Jesus, help."

His response was one I didn't really care for initially. The impression of his words sounded something like this:

"Before you go to the basement, stop and prepare your heart. It will look the way it always looks: messy. Die to the fantasy of having kids who care about cleanliness as much as you do. This is the area the enemy has trespassed to steal your joy and lodge disappointment in you, but I'm going to use it as a training zone to shift your worship back to me."

He was rerouting me back to worshiping him as the source of my peace.

As I type this, I'm wondering how I allowed a whole year to go by before realizing that this was a spiritual battle over my joy!

Whether you are dealing with an emotional trigger like a laundry room, a frustrating relationship, or an addiction of some kind, the next few chapters are dedicated to training you to take back the territory that is rightfully yours in Christ!

WORSHIP IS THE INTENTIONAL DECISION TO GIVE OUR WHOLE SELVES OVER TO GOD AND HIS LORDSHIP!

16

WORSHIP

Imagine you are a soldier getting out of your tent one morning. You feel a little more tired than usual so as you head out for the day, you think to yourself, *I don't have the energy to take my gun with me. It's just so heavy and irritating to carry around. I don't think the enemy will be firing today. If he does, I'll just tuck myself behind Jamie in the bunker.*

Let's hope Jamie didn't think the same thing about you this morning.

We may feel too busy (or perhaps lazy, unmotivated, or ill-equipped) on any given day to carry our spiritual weapons into our everyday lives. As referenced in the last chapter, neglecting the spiritual realm is one way that we can give place to the devil in our own lives (Ephesians 4:27).

Throughout my years of ministry, I've noticed that people tend to become extremely teachable regarding spiritual warfare when they believe they are experiencing unusual torment. When the pain shows up, we *all* tend to care a lot more about finding solutions. When I share with others some of the things I'm about to share with you, they get to work right away because they do not want to spend one more moment in physical, emotional, or mental torment.

> **THEY TOLERATE THESE MINOR DISCOMFORTS AS "NORMAL WAYS OF LIVING."**

However, when it comes to "subtle" things like low-grade depression, fatigue, body aches and pains, chronic illness, repetitive accidents, cycles of frustration with a co-worker, bitter feelings towards a spouse, and so on, some people are not convinced that what I'm saying about spiritual warfare is applicable to them. They tolerate these minor discomforts as "normal ways of living" and let the enemy have his patch of territory saying, "Oh well, that's life." There he is, living it up right under their noses!

It's a trick of the enemy to think we should reserve spiritual warfare for the "big stuff" like addictions, cancer, or financial collapse and give no spiritual thought to things like joy being stolen from us in the laundry room!

Are you ready to learn spiritual warfare?

THE FOUR WS

I want to make this very simple for you. The Four Ws = your warfare template.

- W = Worship
- W = Word
- W = Weapons
- W = Warrior

The remainder of this chapter will be dedicated to the first "W": **Worship.**

W#1
WORSHIP

The first way that we engage in victorious warfare is to **WORSHIP the King of the Universe.**

Worship is not limited to the songs that we sing at the beginning of a church service. It is not limited to the moment we are on our knees in prayer. Rather, worship is the intentional decision to give our whole selves over to God and his Lordship! In this position, we esteem God to be in the highest position of authority over all!

> **WORSHIP IS THE INTENTIONAL DECISION TO GIVE OUR WHOLE SELVES OVER TO GOD AND HIS LORDSHIP!**

We worship when we intentionally acknowledge him as King over everything. We don't own our money. We don't own our family. We don't own our jobs. We don't own our dreams. We don't own our bodies. We don't own our future. We don't own... anything! Not even our own lives!

Jeremiah the Prophet said,

> "O Eternal One, I know our lives are in Your hands.
> It is not in us to direct our own steps—we need You."
> Jeremiah 10:23 The Voice

In this warfare template, we first position ourselves as surrendered to Jesus' Lordship. It is one thing to "love Jesus" as a Christian, but it is entirely different to make him Lord. Let's be like Jeremiah and place our lives in his hands, under his direction, and admit that we need him!

CONFESS AND REPENT

True worship will bring us to a place of confession and repentance. If we have been in rebellion to God in even the slightest way, we want to admit this to God (confess), then turn around and walk in his ways (repentance). If we don't do this, we aren't under his Lordship and we're still trying to be the god of our own lives.

> If we boast that we have no sin, we're only fooling ourselves and are strangers to the truth. But if we freely admit our sins when his light uncovers them, he will be faithful to forgive us every time. God is just to forgive us our sins because of Christ, and he will continue to cleanse us from all unrighteousness.
> 1 John 1:8-9 TPT

Confession is when we admit that we have sinned against God and his holy standard for us (which is where we receive his protection and blessings for us!). When we have rebelled, turned from God's ways and gone our own way, we have given a place to the devil and have opened ourselves up to being manipulated by him (rebellion is witchcraft, 1 Samuel 15:23). Please understand this: if you have a sin that has you trapped in a repetitive cycle, you will need to go to someone who knows God's word and character and tell them with an eager desire to be free! This is a form of confession.

This type of confession can be frightening because we are ashamed of what we've been doing. BUT, we must lay our shame down (die) and confess it aloud so that it can be brought into the light where it loses its power over us. Secrets that stay in the dark grow and fester into icky, moldy, stinky trash that wreaks havoc on every part of our lives.

If you hear a voice inside trying to tell you, *"This is just a small thing. You aren't hurting anyone by doing this,"* that is a dirty lie. Eventually, our sin will always hurt others. You may not see it openly hurting someone, but if you are acting in rebellion, there will be doors that open in your life and lead to destruction elsewhere. Acting in rebellion will eventually snap and bite the people you love the most. Don't be deceived! If you have something you are struggling with and you've confessed to God but it's not breaking off of you, make the decision to tell someone who will fight with you in loving warfare.

> Confess your sins to each other and pray for each other so that you may be healed. The earnest prayer of a righteous person has great power and produces wonderful results.
>
> James 5:16 NLT

Repentance is when we make a decision in our hearts and even tell God aloud that we are turning around and saying *no* to our own way of living, thinking, acting, and being.

What might this look like? We may suddenly be awakened to our stinky attitude or that we are talking about people divisively behind their backs and covering it up with statements like, "We really need to pray for so-and-so." Or, maybe we realize that we have judged someone in our hearts by assigning motives to them or judging their life. We are forbidden to be the judge of anyone, even ourselves! We tend to judge people by their actions and judge ourselves by our intentions. Neither of these are right and we have not come under Lordship in this area if we find ourselves doing this.

In moments where our hearts become convicted of these offenses, we can humble ourselves and thank Almighty God that he loves us enough to pull us close and invite us to confess and turn the other way! Repentance is simply turning the other way, realizing that we were previously being our own god in that area of our life. When we repent, we are cleansed! It's a supernatural cleansing that requires no more shame or guilt for the sin. We can come out of that confession and repentance as if we've stepped out of a warm, soapy shower with our worship music blazing and smile ear to ear. He not only takes our confession and throws it into the sea, but he cleanses our conscience and now we are under no condemnation - just gratitude!

> He canceled out every legal violation we had on our record and the old arrest warrant that stood to indict us. He erased it all—our sins, our stained soul—he deleted it all and they cannot be retrieved! Everything we once were in Adam has been placed onto his cross and nailed permanently there as a public display of cancellation.
>
> Colossians 2:14 TPT

WARFARE IN ACTION

"Mom!" I heard a loud yell from the living room. This wasn't a normal yell. This was a cry for help. I got up and went straight to the living room where I soon realized that my son couldn't breathe. He was on the verge of tears. I knew immediately that he'd been hit by the enemy. He wasn't choking. It was a full-blown panic attack. He immediately told me that he had been experiencing panic attacks at night and that they had become more frequent during the day.

I know breathing techniques so I was able to ask him to take a calm, cleansing breath, but we weren't stopping there.

With authority, I calmly said, "Let's get this taken care of. God has you, son, and we're going to ask him for help." **This is Lordship. We weren't bowing to fear. We were humbly bowing to God.**

I led him up the stairs to my bedroom and had him sit in my

chair. I asked him to try and tell me what had been going on. I was patient to listen and not rush him. I was not matching his panic. I was in control and holding spiritual authority. (The devil loves for us to come under fear, but remember, Lordship means we don't bow to fear or anything else because we are in his hands and under his care.) I asked what he was feeling physically, what was tormenting him emotionally, and I asked him about sin. He told me what had been eating at him. **This is confession. He stated the things that he knew God wouldn't approve of that were making him feel sad and ashamed.**

I hugged him and told him that I forgave him and that God forgave him. I told him he was a good son and that I admired him for being honest. **This is an important step for confession. He found a loving and safe person he knew wouldn't judge him (because that would be a sin on my part!).**

I asked him to use his own words to ask God for help, admit his weakness, and thank him for forgiving him. **This is the most essential part of confession. He confessed from his own heart and validated it by the words of his own mouth!**

What we did next deserves its own chapter. I am going to give you, what I believe, to be the most critical part of worship that leads to freedom from demonic oppression, curses, and torment.

I will continue with this story in the next few chapters as we move through The Four Ws so that you can trace this real-life example of warfare and victory.

17

WOUNDS FORGIVEN

"Son, is there anyone you need to forgive?" I kneeled next to him as he sat in the chair in my room. I paused and gave him time to think.

"Yes," he answered.

I asked him who he needed to forgive.

"You and dad," he said. The tears started pouring, dropping one after the next onto the carpet.

He then mentioned a friend he needed to forgive. He said that he thought he had already forgiven his friend, but his face came to mind so he must need to forgive him. This is exactly right. Many times, we don't know we need to forgive someone!

I walked him through forgiveness and I want to take you through this same exercise in just a moment. I have walked hundreds of people through this and witnessed people break free from torment, anxiety, bitterness, sickness and of course, broken hearts.

> **BITTERNESS IS DRINKING POISON, HOPING THE OTHER PERSON WILL DIE.**

You may have heard this before, but it is so true: "Bitterness is drinking poison, hoping the other person will die." You see, when we hold judgment, contempt, anger, or resentment against others for what they have done, we have stepped outside the bounds of love and placed ourselves in the judgment seat of God. In doing this, we hold people hostage in our hearts. This isn't Lordship. This isn't worship. This is self-protection and self-worship.

TOTAL FREEDOM MEANS TOTAL FORGIVENESS

We are not the judge. We are to let God be the judge of others, because he is. This can be especially hard when someone has had something devastating happen to them. It can seem impossible to forgive someone who has hurt us, rejected us, abused, or neglected us. But I am here to tell you that your total freedom cannot be found apart from total forgiveness.

Notice that my son had to forgive *me*, his mom, the one ministering to him. He was holding contempt in his heart for me. He told me about a situation where another mom seemed to support her son in an area that I didn't show much interest in and it made him feel that I didn't care about him as much as the other mom cared for her son. The enemy had been pointing out how the other mom seemed to show more love to her son in comparison to me. The enemy had been attempting to plant this seed in his heart: *You're not worth it. You're not interesting. You're not loved.*

In that moment of confession, I could've easily justified my case and explained my way out of being the cause of his pain, but I knew that this moment wasn't about me! It wasn't about me helping his perspective (although I could have gone there very easily) or defending myself or my reputation in his eyes. *It was about his freedom.*

FORGIVENESS BRINGS THE BREAKTHROUGH

After two decades of ministry, this is where I have witnessed the greatest place of breakthrough. If there is a block, especially an emotional or physical block, forgiveness is the key to breaking the dam that's been holding back the flow of the river of God.

Unforgiveness holds people in bondage. You can take that to the bank.

Unforgiveness is the open door that says,

Torment, come on in.

Overwhelm, come on in.

Sickness, come on in.

Depression, come on in.

Anxiety, come on in.

Joy robber, come on in.

Pain, come on in.

Hell, come on in.

There is only one way out of this: we need to shut the door of unforgiveness, hatred, and bitterness towards others.

If you have contempt, unforgiveness, bitterness, judgment, or assumptions about others in your heart, you need to let it all go. ALL OF IT. It is the great toxic thief of the body, soul, and spirit. It steals joy, relationship, creativity, inspiration, energy, positivity... the list goes on! My goodness, if you get anything from this book, get this: you must be brave and forgive, sweet one. No matter what the situation is, you must forgive to be free!

If you want to be spiritually sick, hold on to all the things others have done to offend you. It will kill you. If you want to be spiritually, physically, and emotionally soaring to new heights, free as a bird, then let's do this.

ENCOUNTER THE BLOOD

Be aware that you are going to forgive people by faith. You cannot do it in your flesh. Remember, this whole book is about our flesh dying. The flesh cannot help you here. The flesh wants to be mad, hold grudges, protect you, and so on. IT IS BY FAITH that you will release your offenders. YOU CAN DO IT! I BELIEVE IN YOU!

Let's begin! You can either choose to scan the QR code and listen to me guide you through with my audible voice, or keep reading the following text:

Find a quiet space.

In your mind's eye, think of a place you feel extremely comfortable, happy, and safe. Let yourself get comfortable there. (Pause)

Next, I want you to imagine the cross with Jesus hanging on it. He is bloody and ripped to shreds. Walk up to the cross and look into his eyes. See his love and affection for you. What do his eyes seem to be saying to you? (Pause)

In your mind's eye, take your hand and make contact with his leg. It is dripping with wet blood. Wipe the blood on the palm of your hand, feeling the hair on his legs. This is your Lord, your Savior, your Messiah who has surrendered to the persecution and torment because there is no other way to save you. He chose this punishment so that you could be free of it. The blood should've been yours. The beating and lashing of the metal hooks at the end of the whip should've been for you, but it was transferred to him instead. It's not everyone else's sin, it is yours. And still, his eyes look at you with love. (Pause)

Now, envision a prison in your heart. There are people who are locked up in there, held hostage to what they've done to you. See Jesus hand you a key. With the blood on your hand, you freely take the key and unlock the prison doors and tell everyone to step out of the prison of your heart and mind. Begin to name them aloud, one at a time, telling them to step out of the prison of your heart and be free.

Envision each one of them standing in front of the cross, facing you. Jesus is still hanging there, watching from his place of impending death. With your bloody hand, reach out and place it on the heart of the first person. Looking in their eyes, say these words aloud (literally say this aloud):

_____, *with this blood, Jesus forgave me of all my sins. I sinned against him and I have sinned against others. I have hurt Jesus and I have hurt others. But with this blood, I have been totally forgiven, completely forgiven. Jesus holds nothing against me and forgives me and cleanses me of all sin, every bit of it. I am a child of God, standing perfect in his sight because Jesus cleansed me when he forgave me.* **With this same blood, I choose to forgive you for all of your sins against me.** *I have been forgiven, so now I freely forgive. I was let out of the prison of hell, so now I let you go from the prison of my heart. I free you from all of the judgment I have held against you in my heart. I free myself from the consequences of your choices. You are not my responsibility.*

This is my friend, Jesus. He will take care of you and this situation is up to him. I am free of it. I will leave you here and he will decide what the consequences are. He is my friend and my Lord and I trust him with my life.

Allow yourself to FEEL RELIEF right here. You may cry, you might not, but don't rush through. Wait until you feel the burden lift. You gave it to Jesus and he will supernaturally remove the burden now.

Repeat this for every person you saw in the jail cell of your heart.

Once you have completed this for every person who comes to mind, begin to thank God!

Next, see the empty prison cell in your heart. Ask Jesus to give you a tool to destroy the prison bars, the ceiling, the floor… the entire structure! See Jesus hand you the tool as you begin to tear down and completely remove the prison from your heart. (Pause)

Now that it's gone, ask the Holy Spirit for a replacement.

Holy Spirit, what do you want to put in place of that prison? What gift do you have for me that will occupy that space in my heart? (Pause)

Finally, see Jesus, the resurrected King, up ahead in the landscape in your mind. Walk away from the cross, leaving all of the people there at your back. See up ahead where he is waiting for you, smiling at you, affirming you. Notice the joy on his face.

Notice how proud of you he is. Notice how free you feel! As you approach him, grab his hand and let him take you into the next season of your life. Look up ahead. Do you see anything new? Do you see anything interesting or exciting? He has promised good plans for your life according to his word (Jeremiah 29:11)!

RECORD YOUR EXPERIENCE

Take a moment to record your experience here. THIS WAS A BIG DEAL! You will want to remember this because it is so incredibly life altering. What happened during the forgiveness moment? What did your heart experience? What tool did he give you to tear down the prison?

This will be a monument for you to remember how God gave you the grace to forgive. You have the ability to forgive anyone, anytime! Just walk through this exercise. If you don't have the book and words in front of you, that's okay! It's not the exact verbiage that matters. It's the act of letting them out of your heart, forgiving them with the same blood you were forgiven with, and walking hand in hand with your resurrected King!

What is so special about this type of imagery prayer is that THIS IS REAL. What you just went through REALLY happened in the spiritual realm. You will notice a change in your life because of it. Just you wait!

_____

_____

_____

_____

_____

THE WORD OF GOD IS A LAMP. IT LIGHTS OUR STEPS. IT REVEALS THE WAY OF TRIUMPH.

18

THE WORD

*Your word is a lamp to guide my feet
and a light for my path.*
Psalm 119:105 NLT

Let's move to the second "W" in The Four Ws warfare strategy: **the WORD of God.**

W #2
WORD

Imagine that it is the middle of the night and you are in a pitch black bunker. Bombs are going off all around you. The enemy is coming closer and closer. You know there is a tank close by that you can run to that will provide protection, ammunition, and transportation. If you can get to that tank, you will be out of harm's way and better yet, you will be able to fight back without being in danger. The only thing is, you don't know where it is because it's so dark! All you need is a flashlight to find the tank!

The word of God is a lamp. It lights our steps. It reveals the way of triumph. It walks us out of darkness and into the light.

When my son was in his darkest moment of anxiety (gripping fear), he couldn't think himself out of this place, nor could he distract himself. He needed a LAMP to light the path that would lead to the tank. The enemy was hot on his tail and he needed protection, ammunition, and transportation to get out of the firing zone of the enemy.

Many times, the word of God is referred to in scripture as: "precepts," "promises," "truth," or "instruction." Wherever you see these words being used in scripture, God is referring to his word.

THE WORD IS INSTRUCTION FOR US

How did I know that my son needed to CONFESS, REPENT, and FORGIVE? Because that's what the word of God says we need to do to overpower the enemy and apprehend the victory! These instructions will work for you, too, because THEY ARE ALL INSTRUCTIONS FROM THE WORD OF GOD to overcome the enemy (the devil and his strategies against you).

What does the word of God say about **confession**?

> **Confess** your sins to each other and pray for each other so that you may be healed. The earnest prayer of a righteous person has great power and produces wonderful results.
>
> James 5:16 NLT (emphasis added)

What does the word of God say about **repentance**?

Repentance is a deliberate turning from our own way to God's way. It is a 180-degree change in our direction of heart, mind, attitude, thoughts, and behavior. It is the realization that we are in rebellion to God's perfect way. It's the decision to abandon our way of living.

> **Repent**, then, and turn to God, so that your sins may be wiped out,
> that times of refreshing may come from the Lord.
> Acts 3:19 NIV (emphasis added)

What does the word of God say about **forgiveness**?

> But if you withhold **forgiveness** from others, your
> Father withholds forgiveness from you.
> Matthew 6:15 TPT (emphasis added)

There are many more scriptures on repentance, confession, and forgiveness.

EQUIPPING HIM TO REIGN VICTORIOUS

After my son repented, confessed, and forgave, I prayed for him using some of my weapons to help him combat, and as we worked together, the anxiety stopped and the enemy lost his grip. I'll get to that in the next chapter, but for now, I want to jump ahead and share what we did at the final stages for my son's moment of freedom.

In order for my son to stay free, I knew that he would need the weapon of the WORD in his own possession. I can't show up every time the enemy wants to attack him. My son needs his own dagger in hand and he needs to know how to use it so that he can fight back on his own behalf. The enemy commonly tries to take a second, third, and fourth lap back around…. sometimes more! So, rather than high-fiving and thinking our work was over, we did some equipping and combat training.

The word of God is called a "double-edge sword," which means "double mouthed" (Hebrews 4:12). You see, there are *two* mouths that are both needed to drive the dagger through the enemy: God's mouth and *our* mouth. God has already spoken his living word out loud and that is what we read in the scripture. When *we* speak it out loud, the word becomes a double-edge. Anytime we want to drive the dagger of the word through the enemy to take him out, we need to speak the word of God OUT LOUD.

> **ANYTIME WE WANT TO DRIVE THE DAGGER OF THE WORD THROUGH THE ENEMY TO TAKE HIM OUT, WE NEED TO SPEAK THE WORD OF GOD OUT LOUD.**

Jeremy, a friend and ministry leader of ours, knew this and wisely instructed my son to open his Bible to Psalm 91 and read it aloud with authority.

My son read the following passage of scripture out loud with authority just as Jeremy had instructed him to. (Feel free to practice using this spiritual weapon by reading this passage out loud, as well.)

Psalm 91 NLT

1
Those who live in the shelter of the Most High will find rest in the shadow of the Almighty.
2
This I declare about the Lord:
He alone is my refuge, my place of safety;
he is my God, and I trust him.
3

For he will rescue you from every trap
and protect you from deadly disease.

4

He will cover you with his feathers.
He will shelter you with his wings.
His faithful promises are your armor and protection.

5

Do not be afraid of the terrors of the night,
nor the arrow that flies in the day.

6

Do not dread the disease that stalks in darkness,
nor the disaster that strikes at midday.

7

Though a thousand fall at your side,
though ten thousand are dying around you,
these evils will not touch you.

8

Just open your eyes,
and see how the wicked are punished.

9

If you make the Lord your refuge,
if you make the Most High your shelter,

10

no evil will conquer you;
no plague will come near your home.

11

For he will order his angels
to protect you wherever you go.

12

They will hold you up with their hands
so you won't even hurt your foot on a stone.

13

You will trample upon lions and cobras;
you will crush fierce lions and serpents under your feet!

14
The Lord says, "I will rescue those who love me.
I will protect those who trust in my name.
15
When they call on me, I will answer;
I will be with them in trouble.
I will rescue and honor them.
16
I will reward them with a long life
and give them my salvation.

"How do you feel, son?"

"I can breathe."

Over the next several weeks, and even to this day, my son has had to open the Bible and read scripture aloud. We looked up more scriptures on protection, peace, and overcoming fear. These have become his safe place. He would tell you to this day that he cannot live in peace without the word spoken aloud from his own mouth. At seventeen years old, he has gone from hearing his whole life how important the word is, to *experiencing* it at such a level that he is now utterly convinced that the word is life! You see, the devil hoped he would never discover the power of the spoken word!

Hear me on this: if you speak the word of God out of your mouth with authority into the atmosphere, you will push back spiritual attack. You do NOT have to tolerate oppression, fear, anxiety, hopelessness, depression, suicidal thoughts, loneliness, and so on! Open up the Bible. Declare the word aloud. It's almost too simple! Test this out. See what happens!

Lastly, you don't have to use the word of God only when it gets dark. Open it up EVERY SINGLE DAY and recite it out loud. Watch what happens! Declare it into your atmosphere. It will rearrange and change everything.

THE WORD IS ABSOLUTE TRUTH AND ABSOLUTELY FOR US

What must be understood about the word of God is that it holds the final and absolute truth. The Bible holds the authority of truth over all other proclaimed truths. The word of God can be counted on to light our way so that we don't stumble, fall, and trip through our lives. There is no brighter light or greater truth! The world has its own truth that leads us away from light and into darkness and despair.

"TRUE" VS. THE TRUTH

The world may say something is "true," but the word of God is the final Truth. For example, the world may say that if you love someone, you should give yourself sexually to them. To take it even further: if you want to feel good, the world would say it's okay to use someone else's body for your own pleasure if they consent to it.

It seems logical enough, but what is not being considered is the person's heart, worth, and well-being. We are wired for love and made to be intimately known, not for being used like a robot or for someone else's equipment.

This worldly "truth" contradicts the word of God. The word of God is a light for us - not something that God uses to strip us of fun and good times. The word of God is not in place so that we can be religious and get so-called "brownie points" from God. No, the word of God is written for us so that we can be protected from the enemy's destruction.

For example, God wants us to have a covenant of marriage before we give our bodies to another person. He wants two people to make a vow that they will choose only that one person over all others so that their hearts will be protected and they will be known by that person intimately. Each person was made to be chosen only by one. When my husband chose me, he said no to every other human on the planet to become one with. I was made for that type of worth and so were you.

Why would someone think this is a negative thing? If you are God's daughter and he requires that your boyfriend make a wedding vow that he will not be with any other lovers and that he'll be with you in sickness and in health, that's a man worth sharing your body with! If someone cannot make that vow and wants to keep his options open in case someone "better" comes along, he doesn't deserve to be one with you physically. That's what sexual intercourse is: oneness. We become one flesh upon sexual intercourse (1 Corinthians 6:16).

ALL OF GOD'S INSTRUCTIONS ARE TO PROTECT US AND GIVE US LIFE ABUNDANTLY!

With your physical body comes your heart and your soul. You see, God isn't trying to take sex away from you. He's trying to make sure your heart is tended to, protected, and cared for by someone who won't just use you and throw you away. He knows that who you have sex with, you will become one with. It's YOUR HEART that he is watching over.

All of God's instructions are to protect us and give us life abundantly! He is good. He is not a taker. He is not stingy. He isn't one who doesn't want you to have fun. He wants you to be fulfilled in him and in relationships that won't hurt or abuse you. He's awesome like that. You can trust every instruction he gives you in the word! It is a set up to be sure you are protected and provided for.

If you are reading this and think, *Well, that's great because I've had sex with people who I wasn't married to. Now what?*

You are in good company. That was me. I didn't know my worth and I didn't know I would become one flesh with a person I had intercourse with. I had to do what we've already talked about and I advise the same for you if you are willing.

Here are the steps you can take. Executed with a heart posture of sincerity towards God, you can be restored completely. If you'd like to be made brand new, say these prayers out loud:

Confess:
God, I have had sexual relations outside of a marriage covenant.

Repent:
God, I was doing my own thing sexually. I want to do it your way. I turn from my own ways.

Break Soul Ties:
When we give ourselves to someone emotionally, spiritually, or physically, we often develop a soul tie with them. Soul ties can be healthy if this is our spouse. When the soul tie is unhealthy, we can feel pulled in odd directions even if we haven't seen them or talked to them in years! When our soul is "tied" to another in an unhealthy way, we need to break the soul tie.

Imagine a bungee cord connected between you and someone you have had sexual intercourse with, or even a friend you've shared yourself with at a deep level. If there's a soul tie, then, when you move a certain direction in your life, that person will feel pulled toward you (and vice versa). You can find yourself unexplainably devastated or unable to function when the other person experiences something difficult. Even though it is not your challenge, you feel as if it's happening to you!

Does this description sound familiar? If it does, let's break those soul ties. Simply repeat this prayer out loud to sever a soul tie made between you and each person you believe you have one with.

God, I sever myself from the soul tie with _____. I give back what belongs to them and take back what belongs to me. I plead the blood of Jesus over them and myself. I thank you for forgiving me for acting in my own ways of living rather than obeying your word, which is to help me, protect me, and to give me life. In Jesus' name, amen.

Pray this prayer for every person whom you've had any emotional or physical tie to. Even places where you feel that a friendship has been manipulative or you feel obligated to someone else's life in any way, shape, or form. We can accidentally form soul ties with all kinds of people in our lives, not just sexual partners. If you have unhealthy boundaries that display manipulation or consistent worry, break the soul tie and give that relationship over to God as an act of trust.

I have two exercises for you before we move to the next chapter:

1. Open your Bible to Psalm 121. This is a short chapter. Read it aloud and feel the atmosphere of your heart and mind shift!
2. Open your Bible to Psalm 119. This is an entire chapter about the word. Read it aloud and see how it ministers to you regarding the significance of the word of God. Highlight, underline, or circle words that jump out at you.

19

WEAPONS: WARDROBE PART 1

Over the next few chapters, let's unpack the third "W" in The Four Ws warfare strategy: **Weapons.**

W #3
WEAPONS

If we are in a war, it only makes sense that we need weapons in order to be adequately equipped for battle. There are several weapons we will discuss, but the first one I want to point out is the weapon that we wear spiritually. It's our armor!

The Apostle Paul gave us specific instructions for spiritual warfare in Ephesians 6:11-13. Look at these three verses from The Passion Translation:

11 *Put on God's complete set of armor provided for us, so that you will be protected as you fight against the evil strategies of the accuser!*
12 *Your hand-to-hand combat is not with human beings, but with the highest principalities and authorities operating in rebellion under the heavenly realms. For they are a powerful class of demon-gods and evil spirits that hold this dark world in bondage.*
13 *Because of this, you must wear all the armor that God provides so you're protected as you confront the slanderer, for you are destined for all things and will rise victorious.*

DEMON-GODS

Why must we wear all the armor? Look back at verse 12. It says that our hand-to-hand combat is not with human beings, but with the *highest principalities and authorities operating in rebellion under the heavenly realms.* It says that they are *a powerful class of demon-gods and evil spirits* that hold this dark world in bondage.

Your battle is not with your spouse, your co-worker, your boss, or your church leader.

Your battle is not with your landlord, neighbor, or government officials.

Your battle is with the demonic realm!

Look at verse 13 carefully. Because our battle is with demonic enemies, it says that we must wear all the armor that God provides for us so that we're protected as we confront the slanderer. It says that we are destined for all things and *will rise victorious!*

Some Christians don't believe we fight against demonic spirits. This tells me that they haven't read this portion of their Bible. Either that, or they don't really believe the Bible is the highest Truth. Satan would like nothing more than for you and me to fight each other instead of him. The natural weapons of verbal fighting, arguments, bickering, gossip, tattle-telling, rumors, control, manipulation, hatred, and slander are what he hopes we will turn to when we're in the heat of the battle.

For example: he wouldn't want a wife to use the spiritual weapon of faith to extinguish the fiery dart he launches at her that says, *"Leave your husband. There is someone out there who will make you happier."* He wants us to fight each other so that we cannot stand united. United we stand. Divided we fall.

> **SATAN WOULD LIKE NOTHING MORE THAN FOR YOU AND ME TO FIGHT EACH OTHER INSTEAD OF HIM.**

One way he can get us to turn on each other is to make us believe that he doesn't exist. If you don't see the real enemy, you might be fooled into fighting the people around you. Don't go another day believing that people are the source of your battles. The enemy might be using someone as his puppet to come against you, but evil is ultimately coming from him. *He* is the source of evil, not the person he is puppeteering.

SPIRITUAL BATTLES REQUIRE SPIRITUAL WEAPONS

He knows that natural weapons won't defeat him. He also knows that spiritual weapons *will* defeat him.

When it finally occurred to me that I could not fight a spiritual battle with natural weapons, I put down reasoning, logic, blaming, bitterness, control, gossip, aggravation, frustration, and all of those other carnal weapons. None of those could wage war against my real enemy in the battle, Satan. I learned to pick up my spiritual weapons instead. That's when I started winning and **rising victorious** as we just read in Ephesians 6:13. I saw real change in my life when I started taking the spiritual realm and the weapons available to me seriously.

Our spiritual weapons start with Paul's instructions to put on the armor of God.

> Stand your ground, putting on the **belt of truth** and the **body armor of God's righteousness.**
> For **shoes**, put on the peace that comes from the Good News so that you will be fully prepared.
> In addition to all of these, hold up the **shield of faith** to stop the fiery arrows of the devil.
> Put on **salvation as your helmet**, and take the **sword of the Spirit**, which is the word of God.
> Ephesians 6:14-17 NLT (emphasis added)

BELT OF TRUTH

A proficient personal trainer will know that the core must be strong for the entire body to be strong. He or she will spend time making you do core planks and abdominal work so that your extremities can execute strength to their greatest potential.

This scripture tells us that TRUTH is the belt that's wrapped around our core, giving strength to our entire being. I have heard it said that by the time we are five years old, we have 50 percent of what we believe about the world embedded into our core beliefs. By the time we are eighteen years old, it is said that 95 percent of what we believe is wrapped into the core of our belief system.

This is frightening, quite honestly. Many of us weren't taught the TRUTH of God's word. Instead, we made our own observations of the world around us, listened to whatever we were told in school, listened to what our friends said was true, and believed what the media told us. Most of us believed a person's slander against us, as well. "You're ugly; fat; stupid; unwanted."

We have some unraveling of lies to do if we are going to be strong against the powerful class of demon-gods! The only way to unravel a lie is to first be able to identify the lie and then replace it with the TRUTH found in God's word.

How do we unravel a lie if we don't know we're believing one? Think about this! We do this the same way counterfeit money is discovered. You and I probably couldn't spot counterfeit money. It looks and feels like every other bill we have in our wallets!

How can a person in this line of work tell the difference between the "lie" and the truth? They do not study false paper money or coins. They only study REAL money. They study it so intricately that they know every square millimeter of the paper or coin. As long as they know what real money looks like, they are able to spot a bill or coin that doesn't match up with the real thing.

If a co-worker doubts my ability to lead the team, I can easily spot that as a counterfeit because I know the TRUTH about me. God says that I can do all things through Christ who strengthens me (Philippians 4:13). Because I truly believe at my core that I can do all things that God has asked me to do, I'm not discouraged by their opinion. The enemy has lost the chance to use my co-worker to discourage and offend me.

Also, because I know the TRUTH that I'm fighting against demon-gods and not human flesh (Ephesians 6:12), I'm not one bit mad at my co-worker. It's not them I'm fighting.

WE MUST KNOW THE TRUTH AND HAVE IT EMBEDDED IN THE CORE OF OUR BEING!

Do you see how TRUTH anchors us and now the enemy has an impossible time trying to tear us down with lies? WE MUST KNOW THE TRUTH AND HAVE IT EMBEDDED IN THE CORE OF OUR BEING! This only comes from reading and meditating on the word of God to totally reform how we think:

> Stop imitating the ideals and opinions of the culture around you, but be inwardly transformed by the Holy Spirit through a **total reformation of how you think.** This will empower you to discern God's will as you live

a beautiful life, satisfying and perfect in his eyes.

Romans 12:2 TPT (emphasis added)

When my son said fear was on him during the anxiety attack, I had the TRUTH ready to give him in place of that lie.

"Son, God has not given you a spirit of fear, but of power, love, and a sound mind. Do you believe that?" (This TRUTH is found in 2 Timothy 1:7.)

"Yes."

BODY ARMOR OF GOD'S RIGHTEOUSNESS

The purpose of this piece of armor is to protect the heart. Righteousness sounds like a religious word, but in simplest terms, it is our "right standing" with God.

Think about getting in trouble with your mom or dad as a kid. You didn't want to look them square in the eyes because you knew you weren't in "right standing" with them. This caused a separation and the desire to get away from them.

God wants us to protect our hearts from the blows of the enemy (mainly this comes in the form of lies he wants you and me to believe are true) by realizing that we are in right standing with God, the King of kings! We can look at him squarely in the eyes and see his affirmation for us.

GOD LOOKS AT US AND SEES HIS PERFECT SON INSIDE OF US. IT'S MIRACULOUS!

How can this be since you and I have sinned against him? When we repent, turn to God and receive Jesus as our Lord and Savior, those sins are WASHED CLEAN. The debt of our sin has been cancelled by the death of Jesus. Those sins have already been punished. God looks at us and sees his perfect Son inside of us. It's miraculous!

If the devil can convince you that God is mad at you, then you will want to separate yourself from God. Turning our shoulder or back to God will leave our hearts exposed to the enemy. This is where shame opens us up to be duped into doing foolish things. You must know that your shame was dealt with at the cross and your heart is protected here because God sees you as his son or daughter. Not only is God NOT upset with you, he's absolutely crazy in love with you!

> He canceled out every legal violation we had on our record and the old arrest warrant that stood to indict us. He erased it all—our sins, our stained soul—he deleted it all and they cannot be retrieved! Everything we once were in Adam has been placed onto his cross and nailed permanently there as a public display of cancellation.
> Colossians 2:14 TPT

SHOES OF PEACE

I believe that the shoes of peace are not only our instruction to carry and walk in peace and freedom from worry, but they're also our assurance that we have peace with God.

If I am feeling at odds with God, then I am open for attack from the lies of the enemy. He can talk me into feeling ashamed and anxious about my identity and worth. But if I know *at my core* that God holds nothing against me, I can walk in oneness with him. There are no cracks from the enemy that I will slip into! (See Colossians 2:14 above.)

If I am walking in worry, I don't have peace. But, look what happens if I'm "not worried about a thing" and take my requests to God:

> Don't be pulled in different directions or worried about a thing. Be saturated in prayer throughout each day,

offering your faith-filled requests before God with overflowing gratitude. Tell him every detail of your life, then God's wonderful peace that transcends human understanding, **will guard your heart and mind** through Jesus Christ.

       Philippians 4:6-7 TPT (emphasis added)

Isn't it powerful to think about waking up everyday, dead to your own selfish desires and getting spiritually dressed for battle with truth (the belt), righteousness (the breastplate), and peace (the shoes)?

We still have several more pieces to our spiritual wardrobe! Let's continue.

WE CAN'T LEAN ON OUR OWN UNDERSTANDING IF WE WANT TO LIVE IN THE MIRACULOUS.

20

WEAPONS: WARDROBE PART 2

Let's continue taking inventory of our warfare wardrobe.

SHIELD OF FAITH

I love what this piece of armor does: it extinguishes the fiery darts of the enemy! It's critical that we don't believe what we see, but what God tells us is true. This is faith! This can be challenging for many people because we want to believe that truth is something we can see and understand.

> … for we live by faith, not by what we see with our eyes.
> 2 Corinthians 5:7 TPT

> Trust in the Lord with all your heart;
> do not depend on your own understanding.
> Seek his will in all you do,
> and he will show you which path to take.
>
> Proverbs 3:5-6 NLT

This way of living has been the joy of Bob's and my heart for several decades. Believing in God to do something that our minds and skill sets can't manufacture is so much fun! I believe that you and I are wired to live by faith, deeply trusting in our Heavenly Father who has good and exciting plans for us.

One of my favorite stories of believing God for what we couldn't see or understand took place in 2019. We had just lost our business and God was leading us to purchase our retreat center. He allowed us to come under contract with the owners of the property and they miraculously agreed to carry the loan even though our business and income had recently crumbled.

We had some personal savings, so we knew we would be able to come up with the down payment of $215,000. But, something strange happened. Bob woke up to a strong message from the Holy Spirit that we weren't to use our own personal finances for the down payment. The Holy Spirit impressed on Bob that if it was truly God's will for us to have this property, then God himself would come up with the money. There was just one major problem! This was three days before the closing and the transfer of the down payment! We had never believed God for $215,000 in three days before!

We gathered our ministry team and told them what we believed he was telling us. We asked them what we should do and everyone unanimously agreed to fast and pray for three days. We fasted so that our flesh couldn't steal our faith. Flesh wants to understand. Fasting weakens the flesh.

With one day left, our church gave an incredible offering of $23,000 towards the vision at our service. They didn't even know what God had told us! A guest speaker spontaneously called for the financial support of the retreat center and Bob and I watched as dozens of people laid money on the stage. We were in awe.

The next day, with one hour and twelve minutes until closing time, a woman on our ministry team received a text from a friend out of state. Without her ever knowing the details of what we were believing God for, she said that the Holy Spirit had laid it on her heart to support this vision. He gave her a very specific number to give: $192,360 to be exact!

When we added $23,000 to $192,360, we had exactly $215,000 plus $360 for closing fees. What?! For the next forty-eight hours, Bob and I just cried and cried. God blew our minds.

I have many stories like this. I couldn't record them all in one book! Living the life of faith is absolutely wonderful. The key is spending time with the Holy Spirit and reading the word of God so that we can truly know when he speaks. We don't use faith as a random superpower to get what we want in life. That's not how it works. Faith is for the purpose of believing God so that what he says through his word and through his voice of instruction can be trusted even though we can't see it.

It isn't much different when we're in a battle. We decide to believe that we will rise victorious through the care and nature of our great God rather than crumbling under the circumstances we can see. There are countless stories in the Bible where people are celebrated and recognized for believing God for what they could not understand or see! God promised Sarah that she would have a baby when she was already far past child-bearing years! He promises some crazy stuff that doesn't make any sense…that's why we can't lean on our own understanding if we want to live in the miraculous. Let's look at 2 Corinthians 5:7 again.

> … for we live by faith, not by what we see with our eyes.
> 2 Corinthians 5:7 TPT

I've encountered many Christians who only want to do or believe what they can understand. This is a trick of the enemy to get them hit by the fiery dart. When we use the shield of faith, we are choosing to lean on who God is and what he has promised us instead of leaning on our own logic or understanding.

When Peter heard Jesus call him out of the boat to walk on water, he responded with faith. He set both feet on the water and started walking. He didn't say, "Jesus, I'll come out there. But first, I need to understand how I'm going to be held on top of the water without sinking. As soon as I understand it, I'll be right there." You see, Peter trusted Jesus, not his own understanding.

Are you letting trust in your own understanding get in the way of trusting God for your miracle? It's time to pick up your shield of faith!

HELMET OF SALVATION

This is the protection of our minds. The enemy's battlefield is in the mind. If he can get a thought brewing that is laced with a lie, we're going down.

WHAT WE AGREE WITH BECOMES OUR REALITY.

Agreement with a lie is what the enemy wants from us.

A few days after my son got free from the panic attacks, he texted me a thought that came to his mind: "Psalm 91 is the only scripture you have that will work. There aren't any others."

AGREEMENT WITH A LIE IS WHAT THE ENEMY WANTS FROM US.

If you know the Bible, you can basically laugh at this like I did. The enemy wanted my son to stop searching for other scriptures that would muzzle the enemy and allow my son to continue walking in his freedom. I texted him several other scriptures and told him to google "warfare scriptures."

The helmet is to block the lies and this is why we need to put it on! Don't let any old thought find a home in your mind.

I've often described thoughts like sushi boats. If you've ever been to a sushi restaurant that has the conveyer belt or moving water to carry the small plates of sushi, you know that when a piece of sushi moves past you at the table, you look at it and then decide if you want to buy it. If you reach out and take the plate, then you pay for that piece of sushi. You may try it and not even enjoy it, but that's too bad. If you take it, you pay for it.

THE ENEMY WANTS YOU TO THINK THAT BECAUSE YOU THOUGHT OF IT, YOU HAVE TO OWN IT, EAT IT, AND DIGEST IT.

Thoughts are like that. You get thousands of thoughts a day that fly past your mind. The enemy wants you to think that because you thought of it, you have to own it, eat it, and digest it. He knows that this will cost you. You probably need to let most of your thoughts pass on by. Don't reach for any thoughts you don't wish to pay for. You will pay for them.

For example, if you have the thought that you are fat and start thinking about how terrible you look and then start getting concerned and insecure about yourself, it will cost you. You may not pay for it in actual money, but you will pay for it in your joy, your freedom, your confidence, and the list goes on.

One of the most terrible ways to pay is to engage in behavior that reinforces the thought. In this case, overeating or cycles of dieting. When we believe in a lie, we start engaging in behaviors that reinforce the lie. THIS IS THE DEFINITION OF BONDAGE. Yikes!

Can you see how this works? Just because the thought comes to you doesn't mean you have to take it as yours. Is God the author of that thought? If God didn't author the thought, then he doesn't authorize it. It's an imposter and you must take authority over the enemy sneaking into your mind!

Imagine that you are out and about in public. You open your bag and you're shocked to find that a mouse is in there. Would you think, *"Oh shoot. Since that mouse is in my purse, it must be mine to take care of."* No, of course you wouldn't. You would capture it and get it out of there! It wouldn't matter how it got there. You wouldn't need to understand why it was there or how it got there. You would just want it GONE.

The Bible says it this way:

> We can demolish every deceptive fantasy that opposes God and break through every arrogant attitude that is raised up in defiance of the true knowledge of God. We capture, like prisoners of war, every thought and insist that it bow in obedience to the Anointed One.
>
> 2 Corinthians 10:5 TPT

SPIRIT-SWORD

"Take the mighty, razor-sharp **Spirit-sword** of the spoken word of God" (Ephesians 6:17 TPT, emphasis added). "Spirit-sword" is the Greek word machaira, which is a razor-sharp Roman sword used in close combat.

This is what I've come to learn about the enemy. Sometimes he's trying to torment us from far off and then other times, it really heats up and I'm in close combat. He's moved in real close with aggression and I'm at risk of feeling suffocated by his proximity.

My friend, Cynthia, used to be a police officer and said that she was trained to use a dagger in the case that she had to fight someone in close combat. She used this analogy to explain the word of God. When the enemy is breathing down your neck, you'd better pull out the dagger that we talked about a few chapters ago and go. to. town. That is: begin to annihilate him with the spoken word. This is what my son has to do anytime his breathing shifts and he feels his heart begin to race.

When his attack happened, I was absolutely calm. I knew exactly what to do because I know these weapons and I know they work. It was simply a matter of getting him to use them on his own with his own mind, heart, and mouth. I knew that if he would speak the word aloud, arming himself with the full armor of God and engaging in the next weapon that Paul describes, then he would be free.

Dressing for battle is not only powerful, but it is intentional and necessary if we are going to live out our lives in victory. We have an enemy that wants to steal our victory in any way he can, but we should never be intimidated by this! We have the clear instructions in the word of God and the authority given to us by Jesus Christ to be able to win *every single battle.*

We are almost dressed for battle. However, our WARdrobe would not be complete without the most powerful piece (or, perhaps I should say "peace"): **Holy Spirit. He has never lost a spiritual battle . . . and he's living inside of YOU.**

WHEN WE'RE IN A SPIRITUAL BATTLE, WE DO NOT KNOW WHAT TO PRAY. THE HOLY SPIRIT OFFERS US HELP.

21

OUR WARRIOR: THE HOLY SPIRIT

Yes, we have done quite a bit of work in regards to spiritual warfare in the previous chapters, but we're not quite done with the spiritual warfare conversation! We've finally arrived at the most fundamental component for attaining victory: **Our Warrior - The Holy Spirit.**

W #4
WARRIOR

In 1942, our world was at war. The US Marines realized they would need a code that the enemy couldn't crack in order to securely transfer information back and forth at high speeds. This language was life or death to them and would determine their victory or defeat. They turned to the Navajo tribe to help them create a language impossible for outside enemies to decipher and the rest, as they say, is history.

You and I have access to a language just like that through the Holy Spirit, the Warrior of all warriors.

Looking back at the passage in Ephesians that we've been studying, we see further instructions. After putting on the full armor, here is what we do next:

> **Pray passionately in the Spirit**, as you constantly intercede with every form of prayer at all times. Pray the blessings of God upon all his believers.
> Ephesians 6:18 TPT (emphasis added)

What does it mean to "pray in the Spirit"? This means that we allow the Holy Spirit to pray to the Father in us and through us. When we give our lives to Christ, he sends his Holy Spirit upon us, to live and dwell on the inside of us with power!

Jesus said these words right before he was taken up to heaven:

> "But **I promise you this**—the Holy Spirit will come upon you, and **you will be seized with power.** You will be my messengers to Jerusalem, throughout Judea, the distant provinces—even to the remotest places on earth!"
> Acts 1:8 TPT (emphasis added)

When the Holy Spirit prays to the Father on our behalf, it comes from his power in us, not from our own ability. If we are willing, he will use our voice to pray using an unknown language. The language he uses is not our native language. It is a language that you won't understand and the enemy won't either. This is similar to the strategy of the US Marines when they used a secret language that the enemy couldn't understand in order to securely transfer information at high speeds! It is a powerful weapon!

The Bible is clear that the Holy Spirit chooses our bodies as his temple when we make Jesus Christ our Lord and Savior. When we allow him to use our voices and our mouths, the Holy Spirit will pray through us using words that only God can understand. This language allows us to talk to God directly, no distractions or thoughts that are not in line with God's thoughts. It is literally the perfect prayer.

> For if you have the ability to speak in tongues, you will be talking only to God, since people won't be able to understand you. You will be speaking by the power of the Spirit, but it will all be mysterious.
>
> 1 Corinthians 14:2 NLT

In this verse, Paul explains that praying in tongues during gatherings won't be understood by the community unless there is a person to interpret the language (which is also a gift of the Holy Spirit, 2 Corinthians 12:4-11). He contrasts the effectiveness of encouraging others using the gift of prophesy (verbalizing what God is saying using the *native* language) with the mysterious language of praying in tongues.

However, he wasn't doing away with the heavenly language! Paul said that he prayed in tongues more than anyone (Corinthians 14:18)!

Look back at Ephesians 6:18 above. It says to pray in "every form of prayer at all times." Praying in our known language *is* effective, but when we don't know what to pray, we can pray in the Spirit. Often, especially when we're in a spiritual battle, we do not know what to pray. The Holy Spirit offers us help.

> **WHY WOULDN'T HE TRY TO DE-WEAPONIZE US IF HE'S ABLE?**

Some people don't believe that tongues are for today. I can see why the enemy would want us to believe that. Why wouldn't he try to de-weaponize us if he's able? Praying in tongues is like a machine gun to the head for him.

A religious spirit wants the Holy Spirit to be *separate* from us. It says we need to do good things to have a good life and get in good graces with God.

However, Jesus never told his disciples to do enough good things to have a good life. In fact, he told them exactly where their power would come from before he ascended into heaven. He gave them specific instructions *not* to go out into the world *until the Holy Spirit had come upon them in power.* He knew that they could not build the body of Christ without the power and boldness that the Holy Spirit would give them.

Let's look at this scripture one more time, noticing that the power was given to us so that we could be his messengers all over the earth! Without this power, we won't have the boldness and authority it takes to share our message with a hurting world.

> "But I promise you this—the Holy Spirit will come upon you, and **you will be seized with power. You will be my messengers** to Jerusalem, throughout Judea, the distant provinces—**even to the remotest places on earth!**"
>
> Acts 1:8 TPT (emphasis added)

Satan's plans are intersected and demolished when we pray. If we truly believe the Bible is the final TRUTH, then we will take Ephesians 6:18 seriously and pray in the Spirit with power! After activating your prayer language, don't be surprised when you feel the deep unction to go tell a hurting world about your love for God!

THIS IS FOR THE CHILDLIKE

My son will tell you that he speaks in tongues to align himself with the Prince of Peace. All of my kids began to speak in tongues as soon as they were saved. Now, they didn't have the discipline to pray on a consistent basis (let alone pray in tongues) until they were older and life presented pressures. Sometimes we do not devote ourselves to a consistent prayer life until we've run into some problems trying to do it on our own. The more pressure the day presents, the more communion (prayer) with God we realize we need!

Praying in tongues is not an elite "upper level" gift. In fact, I was filled with the Holy Spirit in my young twenties and went on to experience some of the darkest days of my life caused by my own sin. When I *was* praying in tongues daily, I was grounded and in incredible oneness with God, but then I got distracted by the world and left church, left the people who wanted to disciple me, and left prayer. Basically, I left God.

At any moment during these dark times, I could've spoken in tongues because the Holy Spirit was in me. However, there was an entirely different problem at hand: I WASN'T DEAD TO MYSELF. (You can read my testimony in my book *Still: Seven Ways to Find Calm in the Chaos*.) I lacked discipleship and didn't know the word of God at all. When I was in the height of my sin, I wasn't calling on the Holy Spirit to hang out with me.

There came a day when I came to my senses. Leaning over a toilet, hungover from the night before, I told God I was done living my life my way. The pain of my rebellion had caught up to me.

He was right there. I could feel the Holy Spirit behind me as if he was standing there in the flesh. I heard him say, *"Are you ready to move on from this?"* I could tell that he had a plan for my life that was very different from my lifestyle of partying and filling voids with alcohol.

That was twenty years ago and I have not used alcohol to numb myself from that point forward. That's because of his power, not mine. I have no power of my own and my life is proof of that. The Holy Spirit walked me through healing from childhood wounds, which was why I was using alcohol to escape, and he has been my *very best friend* ever since.

I say all this to emphasize that speaking in tongues is a wonderful and powerful gift, but it is just that: a gift. It is not a denomination. It is not a style of Christianity. It is not an indicator of our spiritual maturity. It is a powerful way to stay connected to the Father and is incredibly effective when it comes to demolishing the enemy.

GO ALL IN

Consistency is the key. To think we just pray in tongues a few times and "check the box" that we are filled with the Holy Spirit is missing the point entirely. The Holy Spirit is a person, not an "it." He is not a mist or a cloud. He is a person and part of the trinity: the Father, the Son, and the Holy Spirit. As we spend time with him in worship, in the word and in prayer (conversation), we get to know him and become one with him. Our "doing" isn't the point. Being IN HIM and him IN US is the goal. Oneness.

Being baptized in the Holy Spirit means you are giving the Holy Spirit permission to come upon you with power like Jesus told his disciples in Acts 1:8. Baptism means "full submersion." When we are baptized in the Holy Spirit, we are being fully submerged with his Spirit and allowing him to be in us to overflowing. The Holy Spirit comes with many gifts (see 2 Corinthians 12:4-11) and praying in tongues is one of them.

If you want to be baptized in the Holy Spirit and pray in tongues, then simply pray this prayer or use the QR code to let me guide you through this powerful moment:

Lord Jesus, baptize me with your Holy Spirit. Fill me up to overflowing within. I surrender to your power and most importantly, I make Jesus Christ the Lord and Master of my life. I surrender my mind, voice, and mouth to you so that the Holy Spirit may pray through me and intercede for me. Amen.

Now, as a way to focus, place one hand at the top of your stomach, right where your ribs begin. This is where the Spirit will pray from. Fix your mind on Jesus, his goodness and his majesty. Open your mouth and let the sounds from your inner being come out. Sometimes they sound like groans. You may sound like a baby babbling at first. That's common. Stay present in your worship and let the sound pop up and out of your mouth. Stay focused on your innermost being where your hand is placed, shifting away from a "heady" intellectual place. Simply let the sounds take shape around your tongue and leave your mouth. It won't be a word you recognize or understand. Let it happen.

As these sounds come out of you, notice how your spirit feels. One hundred percent of the time, when I ask people how their spirit feels when they pray in tongues, they confirm that it feels right, it feels like peace, and they feel connected to God.

Afterwards, it's common to hear in your mind, *"That wasn't real. That was stupid."* This is the enemy trying to get you to never do that again. Don't buy into his lies. Pray in the Spirit constantly, every single day, multiple times a day! You will open up creativity, strategies, and wisdom, not to mention the victory in warfare that you will experience.

THIS IS LIFE AND DEATH

I have to tell you one more story.

I was leading from the front at a retreat in Nashville. We were in a powerful worship session and I was praying over the community. Suddenly, I had this intense urgency (a 911 alert in my spirit) that we all needed to pray for our children in our prayer language.

We started in right away, everyone who prayed in tongues began to pray and others prayed intensely in English. I didn't know what the urgency was for, but I knew that the Holy Spirit had moved us into sudden intercession. After a few minutes, the burden lifted and I felt relief. We simply moved on and no one could say what the intercession was for.

When Bob picked me up from the airport, he told me that he had a scary incident with our seven-year-old daughter. He had taken Esther golfing while I was away and as they approached one of the tees, a ball had come flying past Esther's head, just inches from her temple. A young golfer was out hitting balls and not paying attention. My husband admitted to coming unglued with this young man. When I asked him what day and time it was, it matched up exactly to the moment of intercession we'd had over 2,000 miles away.

If there is something I've learned in all of this, it is that when the burden hits (you feel something off or strange in your spirit that you cannot put your finger on), you immediately begin to pray in tongues until the burden lifts. I have so many more stories I could tell you about this. Stories that have saved people's lives. This is why the enemy hates our prayer language and is committed to dividing churches over the topic, lying to people by telling them it passed away thousands of years ago. That's not what my Bible says!

If you would like more understanding of the relationship you can have with the Holy Spirit, I strongly recommend two curriculums that will walk you through scriptures and lessons on the wonderful work of the Holy Spirit:

1. *The Holy Spirit* by John Bevere
2. *The God I Never Knew* by Robert Morris

Holy Spirit brings such wonderful care to our lives. I can't imagine my life without my best friend each and every day! He sits with me, works with me, creates with me, cleans with me, guides me, corrects me, comforts me, and counsels me. The Holy Spirit is personal and available to you, as well.

He is also the most powerful weapon we have! He is our Warrior! Just let this sink in - he lives in you! Our Warrior, the Holy Spirit, lives and dwells in us, ready for battle! He is inviting us to collaborate with him, contributing our voices and faith to push back the darkness.

Will you work with him, allowing him to be your victorious Warrior, too?

OUR POWER AND AUTHORITY ISN'T ABOUT THE ABILITIES WE HAVE; IT'S ABOUT WHO WE HAVE.

22

WIN THE WAR

"Mom, it's a demon. I know it is. I can feel it."
As promised, I'm circling back to a specific moment during the ministry time with my son. He has witnessed many demons being cast out of believers for many years, so this wasn't new to him. What was new to him was the realization that something had trespassed *his* body. He could feel something in his stomach and he just knew that it was connected to the panic attacks.

I called the demon out by using a name that would describe the torment: "Anxiety, fear, get out of him right now in the name of Jesus! You loosen your hold right now and come out of him. Leave now."

My son stood up from the chair and went to the bathroom a few feet away and threw up. Done.

When someone gets free of a demon, they may vomit, they might sob, or they might have no manifestation that is noticeable. We don't judge a person's freedom based on the way a demon leaves a person. We only care that the person is free. We aren't there for a show and we aren't there to find our joy in the fact that demons obey us. Jesus said that we can rejoice that our names are registered in heaven!

> When the seventy-two disciples returned, they joyfully reported to him, "Lord, even the demons obey us when we use your name!"
> "Yes," he told them, "I saw Satan fall from heaven like lightning! Look, I have given you authority over all the power of the enemy, and you can walk among snakes and scorpions and crush them. Nothing will injure you. But don't rejoice because evil spirits obey you; rejoice because your names are registered in heaven."
>
> Luke 10:17-20 NLT

Maybe you don't believe that demons can get inside a person. This is probably because you've been told that by someone who was told the same thing. Or, maybe whoever told you that doesn't read or believe the Bible. One thing is for sure: they have never witnessed a person getting free of demons or they would be able to testify to this reality.

Or, perhaps you believe that demons only show up in wild, rebellious people with crazy eyes and a disheveled appearance. Though these are indicators of a demonic presence, demons certainly aren't limited to this type of person. No one would look at my son and size him up as a kid invaded by demons. He showers everyday, honors his parents, and pursues Jesus.

Here is the basic reality of demons: they are in the atmosphere, but they prefer to live in a body. It's easier to inflict pain and lies when they have access from the inside. Just like a thief, it's much easier for an employee to steal from an employer because he has access from the inside versus a customer who doesn't have access to the back room, file cabinets, and locked drawers.

Deliverance is the act of driving a demon out of a person's body.

CASTING OUT DEMONS

When I first encountered demons in people, I wanted to react in intimidation because I didn't know that I had more authority through Christ in my little pinky than all of the demons in hell put together.

So do you!

When I started to understand the authority that God had given me through his Son, I realized that it was not a big deal to cast a demon out of someone.

Casting out demons is not about puffing up your chest. It's not a power encounter. It has everything to do with the authority you carry on the inside of you. Legally, demons are required to obey the name of Jesus. They don't have to obey *your* name, but they do have to obey the name of Jesus.

Imagine you are driving on the freeway and a Toyota Sedan drives right up on your bumper and the driver waves his fist in rage at you, then begins to yell, "Pull over! This is a citizen's arrest!" Would you pull over? I would hope not. But, what if a police officer pulled up behind you and turned the siren and lights on? You'd be pulling over if you didn't want to go to jail.

You see, demons are under the rulership of Jesus. How you act towards a demon doesn't kick them out. It's the authority you come in (the name of Jesus) that makes them realize they have to pull over and obey what you tell them to do.

Hell was defeated when Jesus went to the grave. He took back the keys of the kingdom from Satan (keys are authority) and then gave that authority to us. Demons aren't going to "pull over" for just anyone, but they are required to pull over if Jesus Christ commands them to.

When I confronted the demon that was harassing my son, I came in the authority that all demons are required to obey: Jesus.

THE MORE DEAD YOU ARE TO YOURSELF, THE MORE AUTHORITY OF GOD YOU WILL CARRY.

The only way to have access to the authority of Christ is to have Christ living in you. If you have invited Jesus to be your Savior, then you have Christ in you. You don't come in your own name. You come in *his* name. In fact, the more dead you are to yourself, the more authority of God you will carry.

My kids have asked to use my debit card many times. I give them my card and my pin and they go to the store and grab what they need. The card has MY NAME ON IT. Their name is nowhere on the card. The cashier doesn't ask if they've been a good kid and then allow them to use the card if they "deserve to."

In the same way, operating in the authority of Christ has nothing to do with our "goodness" or skill sets. It is simply this: we've made him our Lord, which makes us daughters and sons. Because we're his kids, we have access (authority) to everything that is his. Our power and authority isn't about the abilities we have; it's about WHO we have.

If we confront the enemy in our name or our power, we're done. We will not win. We will get in a big mess. When we come in the name of our *Lord*, the Master of the entire universe who kicked Satan out of heaven for even the thought of wanting others to worship him, we come with all of the authority that Jesus carries. It is authority on loan.

My money isn't my kid's money, but I give them access to it by letting them use a card with my signature on it. I loan it to them and that gives them full access.

The last words that Jesus spoke before he ascended into heaven were these words. I have to believe that he chose his last words wisely and would want us to remember them!

> And then he told them, "Go into all the world and preach the Good News to everyone. Anyone who believes and is baptized will be saved. But anyone who refuses to believe will be condemned. These miraculous signs will accompany those who believe: They will cast out demons in my name, and they will speak in new languages. They will be able to handle snakes with safety, and if they drink anything poisonous, it won't hurt them. They will be able to place their hands on the sick, and they will be healed."
>
> Mark 16: 15-18 NLT

That just about sums it up right there.

THE NAME OF JESUS

"In the name of Jesus" might be a phrase you have heard Christians say. Notice that the disciples were amazed that the demons obeyed them when they drove them out *in the name of Jesus*. Do you know the power of the name of Jesus? Let's see what the Bible says:

> "You can ask for anything **in my name**, and I will do it, so that the Son can bring glory to the Father. Yes, ask me for anything **in my name**, and I will do it!"
>
> John 14:13-14 NLT (emphasis added)

> "At that time you won't need to ask me for anything. I tell you the truth, you will ask the Father directly, and he will grant your request because you **use my name**. You haven't done this before. Ask, **using my**

name, and you will receive, and you will have abundant joy."

John 16:23-24 NLT (emphasis added)

I want to share a story with you regarding the most powerful words you could ever speak: "In the name of Jesus."

URSULA

After I prayed the dangerous prayer, "Lord, make me into an entirely different person," I began to experience so many challenges. I didn't understand that what the enemy was throwing at me, God was allowing in order to set me up for my good and for my advancement.

One of the extremely difficult things that I experienced was losing my voice. For months, my voice was raspy and my vocal cords were inflamed. I preached and taught and kept moving forward, but I felt as if I had ruined my vocal cords somehow.

One day after a church service, a few ladies in our community came up to me and said, "We need to pray for your voice." I had received prayer for this many times, but more prayer was needed until my healing came!

Ironically, "Her Voice" Conference wasn't too far away and I was the leader of the organization. Because I have a mandate to release the voices of women, he was trying to take my voice away. (Hint: The enemy intentionally attacks the areas where we have been anointed to set the captives free.)

At the time, I didn't realize that I was dealing with a demonic strategy. That is, I didn't realize it until I fell asleep that night after the ladies had prayed for me. This was the dream I had:

I saw my old friend - the one who had betrayed my trust. She was walking through a desert like a zombie. She had a large mohawk, earrings in her body everywhere, and black makeup. She was dressed as a rebel. Following behind her were maybe twelve people, all dressed in creepy robes and ragged clothing. They were in a trance, trailing behind her as if they had no mind of their own; no free will.

She was heading towards the edge of a cliff and I knew that if she kept walking, she would go off the cliff and all of the people would follow her. I ran up to her and said, "You're not going to make it alive if you go off that cliff!" The Holy Spirit stepped in before she had a chance to respond to me and gently led me away saying, *"Let her go."* (He was severing the relationship.)

In the next scene of my dream, I saw a fortune teller booth where a woman was impressing many people surrounding her. She was accurately telling them their past in order to gain influence and tell them their fortune.

I saw a woman standing away from the booth, peeking in curiosity. I walked up to her and said, "You don't need that." She gasped back at me, almost offended, and said, "How can you say that? She is so accurate!"

I replied with the question, "Do you have two kids?" Her eyes lit up and she was totally impressed by the fact that I knew something about her that perhaps the fortune teller could have told her.

She responded, "How did you know that?"

"I don't know you, but Jesus knows you." She walked away from the booth satisfied to be known by Jesus. (That's what we all want anyway: to be known.)

I turned around to walk away, completely satisfied with the fact that this woman hadn't been duped by the fortune teller. As I walked away, though, I felt a large, dark presence behind me. Before even turning around to see what it was, I knew I was in trouble.

I turned around to see a large woman in a dark, black cape and grey, swirled-up hair towering over me. It was Ursula from The Little Mermaid! She had large lips and cat-like eyes. She was fuming mad. I instantly knew that she was the ring leader of the fortune-telling district that I had just walked through and she was outraged that I busted up her operation by diverting that woman's attention to Jesus.

Towering over me, she said, "I'm going to kill you!" She lunged at me with a white javelin with a round end that had multiple metal spikes on it. As she lunged at me, I yelled, "In the name of Jesus!" and swung a right backhand against the javelin.

Suddenly, I was being pushed back a few feet and she was gaining ground on me. Uh oh. I didn't have any other weapons. I didn't have a fancy javelin. I just used the only weapon I had, which was the name of Jesus. With my very best, she was still gaining ground on me. I had no idea what to do next.

THIS IS THE NAME ABOVE EVERY NAME.

That's when the Holy Spirit showed up. He leaned into my left ear and said very calmly, *"Now, say that one more time, but this time, say it with THE REVELATION!"*

That is when the light bulb went on in my spirit. That's right! This is THE NAME OF JESUS. These aren't just words that Christians say. *This is THE NAME ABOVE EVERY NAME.* This revelation of who Jesus is and the realization of how his name is the Supreme over all hit my whole being and I swung my right arm at her (which symbolizes authority), yelling with a violent shout, "IN THE NAME OF JESUS!"

Ursula was thrusted back and vanished. Just like that, she was gone.

When I woke up, I turned to my husband in bed and whispered, "I just fought a witch." My hand still hurt from the spikes. I was in close combat with a demon-god, just like the word says, and THE NAME OF JESUS wiped her out.

Here's the fun part: my voice came back. It had been nine months and now it was crystal clear! What?! If that doesn't get you fired up, we need to check your pulse!

Ursula was the sea witch who bartered with Ariel to steal her voice. The first parts of the dream with my friend and the fortune teller booth were showing me where the doors had been opened for Ursula to have access to my voice. Although I love my friend even though she is out of my life now, I realize that the prophetic gift was being used to control, manipulate, and create a following. When I broke up the relationship, Ursula was infuriated because I wasn't playing her games anymore.

In the next several days, I realized that I was in a war. This war wasn't a fantasy. This was real and I wasn't fighting flesh and blood. I had a big helping of revelation on the authority I have through the name of Jesus. Saying the words in emptiness means nothing, but saying the words with the revelation of *who Jesus is* has become my victory.

Although dying and letting go of that relationship was one of the hardest things I've ever had to do, I knew that it was so important to be separated from anything or anyone who was manipulating me by way of their spiritual gifts.

Just because someone has a prophetic gift doesn't mean you have to let them into the deepest places of your heart. It doesn't even mean that they are more spiritually mature than you or that they should mentor you. They certainly aren't allowed to think for you! Ask God for discernment and wisdom, he will give it to you.

Now when I pray for someone, I don't just say, "In the name of Jesus" because it is what Christians say. I say it because his name wins the war.

YOU WILL COME OUT THE OTHER SIDE A CHAIN BREAKER FOR THE PEOPLE IN YOUR LIFE.

23

WAKE UP TO TRUE LIFE

You understand it well now: the flesh has its way and God has his way. You must choose — **daily**! Today's dying is for *today*. Tomorrow morning, you will wake up and get to choose all over again.

> Then he said to the crowd, "If any of you wants to be my follower, you must give up your own way, take up your cross **daily**, and follow me.
> 			Luke 9:23 NLT (emphasis added)

My prayer is that every single day, you will choose to wake up as a dead person, incapable of going your own way and doing your own thing. I want this for you. It is an absolute fact that if you will shed the layer of the outer flesh, then you will rise in your spirit victorious to the life that God designed just for you! It is a special life. It is full of twists and turns, adventures and blessings. It is absolutely worth it!

When you find yourself in the middle of a crushing season, or a season of fermentation where you're waiting on God longer than you wanted to, I want you to know that you are going to come out the other side more potent and more anointed than ever before. The anointing breaks chains off of people. You will come out the other side a chain breaker for the people in your life.

Don't try to escape the crushing. Don't try to escape the breaking or the fermentation. Trust him. He knows what he's doing. What he is doing *in you* is based on his love *for you*. He is *for you*. Don't ever forget that. You can trust him.

I bless you to wake up dead every single day, rising victorious over the enemy in every area of your life!

In Jesus' name! Amen.

Do you want an amplified experience of *Wake Up Dead*?

In *Wake Up Dead: The Masterclass*, I will guide you through the deeper truths of *Wake Up Dead*. Take this course independently or gather friends for an in-home or churchwide Bible study. For more information on the masterclass and other *Wake Up Dead* resources, visit wakeupdeadbook.com or scan here:

APPENDIX

*"And you will know the truth,
and the truth will set you free."*
John 8:32 NLT

Here is a list of scripture references to replace LIES with the TRUTH. One of the simplest ways to find these scriptures is to put the scripture reference in your search engine (example: 1 Corinthians 10:13-14). I like to use the Bible app called "YouVersion." Use this QR code to download the YouVersion app.

After you find the scripture, read it aloud. I highly suggest that you highlight or underline them in a paper Bible once you find the scripture. Even if you used a computer or phone to find the verse, open your paper Bible and underline it. It makes a big difference in how your brain will process and hold on to it.

If you'd like to drive these truths deeper, you can write them in a notebook or on notecards and meditate on them (think on them intently and daily) until they become what you believe. We live out the paradigms we believe (Proverbs 23:7).

NOTE: There are many more scriptures for each topic than what is listed. For more scriptures, type in your search engine, "topic + Bible scriptures," or use this site to search for a list of scriptures by topic: ***https://www.openbible.info/topics/***.

LIE "I am / I feel"	TRUTH
ADDICTED	1 Corinthians 10:13-14; 1 Corinthians 15:33; 1 John 2:16; James 4:7
AFRAID	Isaiah 41:10; Joshua 1:9; 2 Timothy 1:7; Hebrews 13:6; Psalm 34:4
ALONE	Isaiah 41:10; Psalm 25:16-21; Psalm 23:4; Deuteronomy 31:6; Psalm 27:10
ANGRY	James 1:19-20; Proverbs 29:11; Ecclesiastes 7:9; Proverbs 15:1; Psalm 37:8-9
ANXIOUS	Philippians 4:6-7; 1 Peter 5:6-7; Matthew 6:25-34; John 16:33; James 1:5
ASHAMED	1 John 1:9; Isaiah 61:7; Isaiah 50:7; Psalm 34:4-5; Romans 8:1; Psalm 3:3
BROKE	James 4:2; Philippians 4:19; Psalm 37:5; Proverbs 20:13; Luke 12:32-34
CONFUSED	1 Corinthians 14:33; Psalm 119:169; John 16:13; 2 Corinthians 4:8; Proverbs 3:5-6
CRAZY	1 Corinthians 2:16; 2 Timothy 1:7; James 1:6-8; 2 Corinthians 10:5; 1 John 2:15
DEPRESSED	James 5:13; Psalm 34:17-18; Psalm 9:9; Revelation 21:4; Isaiah 41:10
DISTRACTED	Psalm 119:37; Psalm 119:105; Psalm 119:18; James 4:3; Romans 12:2
HOPELESS	Romans 15:13; Jeremiah 29:11; Isaiah 40:31; Psalm 39:7; Romans 8:24-25

IMPATIENT	James 5:8; Psalm 27:14; Psalm 37:34; Proverbs 19:2; Proverbs 21:5; Proverbs 26:10
INADEQUATE	James 1:5; 2 Corinthians 3:5; 2 Corinthians 12:9-10; Philippians 4:13; Philippians 4:19
INTIMIDATED	Joshua 1:9; Deuteronomy 31:6; 2 Timothy 1:7; Proverbs 21:8; Mark 5:36; Psalm 112:7
LAZY	Proverbs 18:9; Genesis 2:15; 2 Thessalonians 3:10; Proverbs 13:4; Proverbs 12:24
NUMB	Malachi 4:2; Ephesians 4:32; Psalm 77:6; Revelation 3:15-17; Colossians 3:23-24; 1 John 4:8
OFFENDED	Proverbs 19:11; Ephesians 4:31-32; Matthew 18:15-17; Philippians 1:9; Romans 3:23
OVERLOOKED	1 John 5:14; Hebrews 6:10; Colossians 3:23; Jeremiah 1:5; Psalm 139:13
OVERWHELMED	Psalm 34:17-20; Matthew 19:26; Colossians 3:2; Matthew 11:28; Philippians 4:19
SAD	Matthew 5;4; 2 Timothy 2:1; Revelation 21:4; Psalm 147:3; Psalm 56:8; John 16:33
SICK	Psalm 91:1-16; James 5:14-16; 1 Peter 2:24; Mark 5:25-35; Isaiah 53:5; Psalm 103:3
STUCK	James 1:1-27; Jeremiah 29:11; Proverbs 15:22; Habakkuk 2:2; 2 Corinthians 12:9; 2 Peter 3:8-9; Philippians 1:6
STUPID	Proverbs 1:7; Proverbs 19:20; Psalm 111:10; Proverbs 17:27-28; Proverbs 11:2
TEMPTED	1 Corinthians 10:13; Matthew 4:1-11; James 1:1-13; Hebrews 2:18; James 1:1-27
TIRED	Jeremiah 32:27; Matthew 11:28-30; Isaiah 40:28-31; Galatians 6:9-10; Jeremiah 31:25; 2 Thessalonians 3:13
UGLY	Psalm 139:14; 1 Peter 3:3-4; 1 John 2:15; Proverbs 31:30; Genesis 1:26; Song of Songs 2:13-14
UNLOVED	John 3:16-17; Colossians 3:14; 1 John 4:19; Romans 5:8; Proverbs 17:17; 1 John 3:1; 1 John 4:16
WEARY	Isaiah 40:31; James 1:2-4; Matthew 11:28-30; Romans 5:3-5; 1 Peter 4:12-13; Galatians 6:9-10; Acts 1:8
WORRIED	Philippians 4:6-7; 1 Peter 5:6-7; Hebrews 11:1; Matthew 6:25-34; Jeremiah 29:11

WAKE UP DEAD

THE MASTERCLASS

Do you want an amplified experience of *Wake Up Dead*?

In this six-week online Bible study, Jenny Donnelly will guide you through the deeper truths of *Wake Up Dead*. Take this course independently or gather friends for an in-home or churchwide Bible study. For more information, visit wakeupdeadbook.com or scan here:

CONNECT

JENNY DONNELLY

 /JENNYDONNELLYSPAGE

 @JENNYLDONNELLY

HER VOICE MOVEMENT

 /HERVOICEMVMT

 @HERVOICEMVMT

TETELESTAI

JOHN1930.COM

18+ FREE COURSES
6+ MASTERCLASSES
CONFERENCES &
RESOURCES

OUR MISSION:
ENCOUNTER. EQUIP. SEND.

HERVOICEMVMT.COM

FIND A
FREEDOM RALLY
IN A CITY
NEAR YOU

OUR MISSION:
LET FREEDOM RING!